LOST CHILDREN

Penny Cross

Velvet Glove Publishing

VELVET GLOVE BOOKS

First published by Velvet Glove Publishing
PO Box 30617
London E1W 1GP

Penny Cross is hereby identified as author of this work in accordance with Section 77 of the Copyright, Designs and Patents Act 1988.

A CIP record for this book is available from the British Library

ISBN 0 9538 3920 6

Typeset and printed in England by F. Crowe & Sons Ltd, Norwich

FOR MY CHILDREN,

and for my beloved husband JW-F who died a few months before publication of this book.

"We use our parents like recurring dreams, to be entered into when needed. They are always there for love and hate."

Doris Lessing

ACKNOWLEDGEMENTS

Without the deepest love and support love of my husband, who tragically died shortly after I completed this book, it would never have been started, let alone completed.

After I lost my children it was my father, stepfather, brother, sister-in-law and many true friends who gave me a reason to go on. Compassionate, caring families, as well as loving friends who naturally extend and enhance one's family, are precious wells of life, strength and vitality, giving one many reasons for going on when life has never seemed bleaker.

If you have such a family you are rich beyond your wildest dreams.

Foreword by

Catherine Meyer,

wife of Sir Christopher Meyer, the British Ambassador to the United States and author of They Are My Children Too: A Mother's Struggle for her Sons

When I read Penny Cross's book, I immediately realised why she wanted me to write the introduction. I was well placed to understand her pain and why she felt she had to write this book.

Although the circumstances were different, we have both been forcibly separated from our children and seen them turned against us. We have both travelled through the same path of despair. We have both shared the same feelings of helplessness and injustice. We have both tried endlessly to search for a meaning to our tragedy. We have both spent our days and our nights worrying about our children's future. When a mother loses her children, whatever the circumstances, a part of her dies and can never come back to life. That, too, we share.

This book is the result of a family tragedy. It relates the suffering of a mother who could never retrieve the love of her children after they were led to believe that she had abandoned them. When Penny left her husband, she did not realise she would end up losing her children's love.

It does not need to be this way. Many parents are able to work out an amicable settlement. But when one parent has all-consuming feelings of anger and revenge against the other, the child finds itself in an impossible situation. It is forced to choose between parents - one of the worst forms of child abuse. All too often, the aggrieved and vindictive parent directly appeals to the child's loyalty, depicting the other parent in a negative light, systematically programming the child against the absent parent. The child finds itself thrown into war between the two people it most needs and loves. Almost immediately, the child comes to believe that it has been abandoned by the absent parent. Traumatised by the loss of one parent, the child's greatest fear is to lose the affection of the other parent. In its effort to keep the love of the only remaining parent, it blocks out the happy memories of the other, replacing them with anger and resentment. This is what psychologists call Parental Alienation Syndrome. It is real. It is what Penny and I have to endure to this day.

Penny did not want to descend into self-pity. For her children's sake, she wanted to remain strong. She wanted to help others through her own experiences. Above all, she wrote this book for her children. This was the only way she had left to communicate her indestructible, boundless love for them. One day, maybe, they will read her words and realise, as anyone who reads this book will, that despite what they have been led to believe, she is and always has been there for them.

Through this book, Penny hopes to make people aware of the effects broken marriages can have on children: above all, to prevent other parents from making rash decisions that can wreck their lives and those of their children.

This is an eloquent and compelling book. It is a must for couples with children. It is an insight into the worst that can happen, and how to avoid it. It is also a well-researched guide to the long-term effects of Parental Alienation and its devastating effects on children.

Catherine Meyer
Washington, D.C.
May 2000

Catherine Meyer, who was born in 1953, carries both British and French passports. She was educated in London at the French Lycée, speaks five languages and received her B.A. from the School of Slavonic and East European Studies. Whilst pursuing her university studies Lady Meyer joined Merrill Lynch, Pierce, Fenner & Smith and became an Account Executive handling discretionary commodity accounts. She wrote a handbook on the mechanism of the London Metal Exchange Option market. In 1980 she joined E. F. Hutton and became one of the firm's top producers. She was the first woman to be invited to their annual Conference.

In 1984, she married a German. After the birth of their first son they moved to Germany. Their second son was born in 1987. During her last year in Hamburg, she represented the distinguished Russian artist, Alexander Zaitsev, and organised exhibitions of his paintings. In 1992, Lady Meyer moved back to London with her two boys. She returned to the City. Her last position was with San Paulo Bank as a Senior Account Executive in Fixed Income sales.

Following the abduction of her children by her estranged husband in 1994, she had to give up her career and dedicated her life to fight for her rights as a mother. While continuing her struggle to gain access to her children, she is also waging a campaign on behalf of all children in a similar plight. In September 1998, she co-chaired in Washington DC with the National Center for Missing and Exploited Children, the first international conference aimed at combatting the abduction of children across international frontiers.

In April 1999, Lady Meyer helped set up the new International Centre for Missing and Exploited Children, of which she is co-chair. The centre was launched at the British Embassy in Washington by the First Lady of the United States, Hillary Rodham Clinton and Cherie Booth, QC, wife of the British Prime Minister, The Rt. Hon Tony Blair, MP. This was followed by a European launch at Sir Richard Branson's house in London, also attended by Cherie Booth, who is the patron of ICMEC. In the last year, she has been invited to give evidence before the Senate Foreign Relations, Senate Judiciary and the House International Relations Committees.

Following the publication in May, 1999 of her book, "They Are My Children Too" (Public Affairs), she has made numerous television appearances including Barbara Walters' 20/20 and The View, Charlie Rose and Larry King Live. As a result of this publicity, she has attracted scores of American parents in a similar plight. This led to the creation of **Parents of Abducted Children Together (PACT)** and the introduction of a concurrent resolution on the floor of the US Senate and the House on 24 March 2000, calling for a better application of the International Hague Convention on Child Abduction by some countries.

Later this year, she will receive the Adam Walsh Rainbow Award given annually to people who make an outstanding contribution to children's causes. She was named by British Airways Business Life Magazine as one of the people who will be remembered in the millennium for her campaigning on behalf of abducted children.

LOST CHILDREN

A GUIDE FOR SEPARATING PARENTS

ESSENTIAL READING FOR PARENTS *BEFORE* SPLITTING-UP
AND FOR PARENTS JUST *THINKING* ABOUT LEAVING

- Preparing your partner and children *before* one parent leaves

- Preventing emotional abuse by one or both parents

- The 'rejected' parent's need for revenge through the children

- Protecting children's lifetime relationships with both parents

- Parental Alienation Syndrome

- The Family Union after divorce

THE OVERBURDENED CHILD

"Divorce almost inevitably burdens children with greater responsibilities and makes them feel less cared for. Children of chronically troubled parents bear a greater burden. They are more likely to find themselves alone and isolated in caring for a disorganised, alcoholic, intensely dependent, physically ill, or chronically enraged parent. The needs of the troubled parent override the developmental needs of the child, with the result that the child becomes psychologically depleted and their own emotional and social progress is crippled."

Deirdre Conway Rand
The Spectrum of Parental Alienation Syndrome (Part 1),
The American Journal of Forensic Psychology,
Volume 15, Number 3, 1997

WARNING

Splitting up a family, regardless of whether parents are married or living together in a long-term relationship, leaves innocent, vulnerable children robbed of security and potentially scarred for life. This book will make you aware of some dangers and help parents think about ways in which they can lessen the emotional damage to children.

One way in which both parents can do this is to actively and positively encourage children to preserve relationships with all the important adults in their family. Are you as a parent prepared to put aside your own animosity or grief and be genuinely prepared to do so?

This book is also for all professionals involved in supporting a family splitting up: solicitors, barristers, judges, court welfare officers, social workers, mediation, conciliation and counselling organisations.

The positive message is that the family will partially recover in time but it may take five years for everyone to work through their guilt, anger or grief during which period children's relationships with one or both parents could become irreversibly damaged.

The death of a family is a real bereavement. Be warned but, above all, be prepared.

Contents

Introduction

On 21 May 1998 nearly two years after I had left my husband, having left my 12-year-old twins and 20-year-old eldest son behind in the family home (my 18-year-old second son was living in a flat a few miles away), my father received a telephone call.

It was from my ex-husband. He told my father quite dispassionately that my eldest son, then 22 years old, had died the previous day after a motorcycle accident.

With great difficulty my elderly father summoned enough courage to tell me this news over the telephone as he lives hundreds of miles away. Whoever believes death is a great leveller in such circumstances is sadly mistaken. My ex-husband lives only a few miles away from me and knew about my son's death within a few hours. What would it have cost him to telephone me or come and tell me face to face that our eldest son had died?

Did spite or perversion bring about such calculating, callous behaviour? What kind of father could gain satisfaction from withholding such information from a mother for 18 hours and then further gratification by knowing this tragic knowledge will have to be conveyed through a grandfather?

I also learnt through my father that my son had apparently made a Will. He had stated his categorical wish to ban me, his grandfather, his step-grandfather, uncle, aunt and cousins from attending his funeral, a family which had supported me without success two years earlier to gain contact with my two younger children through The Family Court.

Many people have speculated on the reasons why a young man would have bothered to make a Will and whether certain influences were brought to bear on his mind to make such a one as he did.

Visiting the lamp post later that day where my son had lain injured the day before, I left flowers, a note and picked up a piece of belt buckle. I went alone to that lamppost each day for five consecutive days at dawn to check whether my flowers had been thrown away, and to talk to my son.

On the morning of his cremation a week later I went out to buy bread, choosing a shop in the next village where I was a stranger. I broke down in front of the shopkeeper after discovering there was not enough money in my purse.

Driving back home, I screamed out my pain in the privacy of the car along a deserted country road as the time of his funeral approached. Then at 10.30 exactly, the time my son's hearse was leaving the family home to make its journey to the crematorium accompanied by a motorbike cavalcade of young biking friends, I began in my own home to make soup for family and friends who were arriving to spend the day with me, people who were banned from attending his funeral 20 miles away.

My son's ashes were collected shortly after his cremation. I have no idea where they are now buried or scattered.

A week later I visited the consultant at the hospital who, with his trauma team, had tried to save my son's life for two hours. I wanted the fullest details possible of all my son's appalling external and internal injuries so that I could lay him to rest in my mind, so I could know how the last minutes of his life were spent and what measures were taken to save him. The consultant gave me this information, pausing every few minutes to ask if I was all right.

A few days later I began arranging a memorial service which would take place in the town where my son had been born. Placing notices in newspapers in my son's home city where he had died as well as in the town where he had been born, I invited everyone who knew and liked or loved him. Fifty people turned up to pay their respects; tributes were read out from his college lecturer, schoolteachers and others who had known him in childhood and young adulthood. My ex-husband, my three other children and my son's newest motorbike friends chose not to attend.

I am lucky enough to have both a father and a step-father with whom I enjoy a close, loving relationship and who, some might think ironically, get on very well with each other. My stepfather had generously supported my former husband after job losses, lending him over the years thousands of pounds, none of which has ever been repaid. Thankfully, my own mother died six years ago, unable to see adored grandchildren turn on her family and me.

This book is dedicated to my children whose physical presence has now been absent from my daily life for over three years. Because I left my former husband, and through being the kind of mother they now say they never liked, they have cut me out of their lives.

Among many things, they accused me of abandoning them. I did not abandon them, just my husband and a miserable, failed marriage which had lasted 25 years too long. Profound grief at losing my children resulted in my writing this book.

I want to warn parents of the potential risks of just walking out on their marriage or relationship leaving ill-prepared children behind in the family home. Perhaps they have found new love with someone else, perhaps they want to make a new life for themselves; perhaps they are suffering from temporary ill health but with the intention of returning sometime to care for the children.

I want to alert all these parents to the real possibility of their children becoming irreversibly brain-washed into believing, if they are left behind, that the parent who left has abandoned them.

I want to warn those parents of the risks of their children being made to believe that they were 'bad' parents, even if they believed they were putting children's highest interests first in leaving them behind in the family home amongst familiar surroundings, possessions and friends.

In other unique and tragic cases, some parents have put their children into care or had them adopted, to limit the potential damage on their children arising from a variety of disturbing circumstances in their own personal lives. Some of these children, too, are suffering from the belief that one or both parents has abandoned them for selfish reasons and, as a consequence, the children have become alienated from them.

The opinions, advice and views are entirely my own – except where clearly stated and referenced – and might not coincide with the professional advice offered by solicitors, advice bureaux or counselling organisations.

This is not a book I wrote out of self-pity. My pity was exclusively reserved for my children for having had to experience the impact of their father's revenge for, what he later claimed, was his public humiliation because I favoured a man twenty years older than he. Any pity remaining I also gave to my children for suffering an on-going programme of emotional abuse and brainwashing by their father which still continues to this day.

But after more than three years of silence from my children, I have an admission to make.

I want to admit my sorrow my children had a mother like me married to their father. As part of my own healing, I have searched my memory and conscience to see what accuracy there might have been in their allegations I was never a good mother, that I was "*harsh and unfair in disciplining them*" and "*frequently bad-tempered*" [extract from Court Welfare Officer's report].

Now, having considered some of the charges, I probably agree with some of them. Other charges, though, were seriously flawed but my 'defence' fell on deaf ears.

The background to my marriage, the character and temperament of two young people who were initially only physically attracted to each other, who came from different backgrounds and who held diametrically opposed ideas on manners or morals, was a relationship doomed to failure.

Two young people who probably wanted to escape from their home lives, who married because the 'nest-making' instinct was strong at 26 years old, who had in-laws on both sides who were either physically or mentally ill was an ill-judged and fatal decision.

Two young people who married then had regular financial strains but decided to have children because we both loved and wanted them. All this contributed to a recipe for disaster which took its final toll on all of us.

My ex-husband's on-going financial irresponsibility and puerile attempts to rectify its negative effects, our continuous and expensive refurbishment over 23 years of houses we could not afford, his occasional bouts of severe ill-health as well as that of his parents, his drinking binges, my working full-time with two children and later part-time with four children, added immensely to a steadily growing mountain of tension for which there was little relief: no regular holidays, no family car and little time off.

My four children are probably right in having charged me with being frequently tired or being bad tempered. I know I was at fault for trying to bring up them up too idealistically so they would have good manners, morals, ambitions, ideals, some of which, selfishly, might have reflected me in a good light.

I was seriously unhappy, during the whole of my marriage, that they had for their role model as a father someone who finally admitted to having "*misused alcohol over the years*" [extract from Court Welfare Officer's report]. It was arrogant, perhaps even conceited of me, to want children of whom I could be proud and not ashamed, as I was deeply humiliated at times by having such a husband as I had. It was an uphill struggle, sometimes a daily battle, when they seemed to admire negative qualities.

Belligerent, boorish, smart aleck, smart-ass behaviour seemed to have far more appeal, even for my daughter. I fought it, unwisely as it turned out. Discourtesy, rudeness, laziness, making fun of people, doing little at home or at school had far more attraction, seeming to gain more points amongst the five of them.

With that perfect vision, hindsight, most of it should have been ignored. They were lovely, lively, engaging children nearly all of the time. I should have been patient, allowing them the chance to mature at their own pace, as my former husband may now be doing, finally in middle age, surrounded by our three remaining children.

This book has been written over three years of self-discovery, having been absent from my children for that period. I did not like recalling some of my mothering memories and understand more fully now some of the reasons my children do not want to know me. Other mothering memories I recalled with pleasure, fondness and gratitude because of a deep self-fulfilment in motherhood which women like me seem to need.

But I could not understand at the beginning why the children totally rejected everything about me when I truly know there were very many happy times we shared. I did not understand, until now, why I have been annihilated and obliterated from their memories into a non-existent person.

As part of the children's own recovery, I'm told they re-formed their family unit, talked openly and honestly at new "family conferences" about my mothering, and apparently discovered they never liked me anyway. They are all getting on with their lives, are settled at school, and I know instinctively are supporting each other and their father in coming to terms with new lives as well as the death of an adored eldest brother. All are, evidently, much happier now I am out of the home. They are better off without me.

Equally, I can at last admit now with complete frankness to being better off without them. Let me rephrase that. We are all relieved of the demands or pressures we imposed on one another. Now that's gone it's a huge relief. Of course I miss them daily and painfully, but we always seemed to be pulling in opposite directions and what sense is there in that? The release we must all feel at being disconnected from mutually imposed demands is part of our healing process, aiding recovery in new lives, dimming memories of a previous life together.

But the trauma I experienced initially of realising slowly and painfully how quickly my children could turn on me, how easily their feelings could be soured, had the force of colliding at speed with a hard, immovable object. Stupidly, foolishly, I believed nothing could come between my devotion to the children and their regard, love or affection for me.

Insanely, I believed in time, once settled into my new home, my children would gradually come to accept the changes and we would continue as we were. My mothering I assumed would continue, because of what I had invested into it over the years.

Naively, I didn't question that leaving their father could impair my relationships with my children in any critical way. It didn't occur to me their feelings towards me could be so vitally affected or so gravely influenced. It would be a very serious disturbance for them of course, but I assumed it would be that very thing, the break-up, against which their anger or unhappiness would be directed, not at me. Prepared to console and support them throughout their misery, I found I was not needed being apparently the reason for it.

How could their perception of me change so radically, so violently, overnight? How could they forget so much and remember so little?

Very, very easily as it turned out. Mothering memories were tossed in the gutter where they remain to this day. They "*could not remember anything nice I did for them*". And frighteningly, when presented with this statement by the Divorce Court Welfare Officer, neither could I.

In panic, my memories froze. I turned to family and friends to ask if they could remember "*anything nice*" I had done for my children and to write it down for me. They wrote down eventful things, routine, insignificant, caring, loving, everyday happenings. Recollection came back, jogging my own memory with the realisation of how much had been forgotten while getting on with daily, mundane family life.

But I soon disregarded most of it as unimportant and insubstantial when words were written which did not come from my children. As a parent how can you write down what you did for your children and for it not to look as if you are trying to impress someone, to influence them into believing you were a good, caring person? The words looked trite, insignificant, contrived. If the children had judged me as having been a bad mother then I must have been. After all they had been living with me. Outsiders cannot see what happens within the private walls of a family home.

I was told my estranged husband had sent a letter to a family member, shortly after I left him, in which he had explained that he had asked the children "*how they would react if she was severely ill or even dying*".

He gave their response:

> "*They have said they do not care if she was already dead and I believe them since I have seen their feelings expressed. I am saddened to feel her children now all wish her dead and I cannot tell you how this hurts me.*"

Perhaps the children's memories too have been frozen and tarnished by their angry, distressed father as well as by their own deep sadness. I believe though that they have been emotionally abused and brainwashed with such accomplishment by their father they truly think they have not been.

A report by Peggie Ward, a member of the Advisory Council of the Professional Academy of Custody Evaluators (PACE) in the United States into the effect of Parent Alienation Syndrome (the creation of a singular relationship between a child and one parent, to the exclusion of the other parent) categorises PAS into four groups: mild, moderate, overt and severe. She believes that:

> *"These children [PAS influenced] have only extremely hostile feelings for the target parent, and no amount of evidence disproving their stated reasons for their hatred will serve to dissuade them... and have incorporated the alienating parent's hatreds, emotions and desires with regard to the target parent such that it is often difficult to discern who is expressing them."*

Perhaps, with maturity and their own eventual experience of marriage, partnership or parenthood, my children as well as other children alienated from their parents in such an extreme form, may reflect on their reactions and behaviour in the aftermath of their parents' break-up. If so, their own memories may thaw, releasing fragments of the happier, positive earlier times leading ultimately to some form of reconciliation. I hope so, for their sakes.

For me it is too late, having accepted and reconciled myself with the knowledge that I shall never see them again, having lost three precious years so far of their presence and, ultimately, the final and irrevocable loss of my eldest and dearly loved son with whom I shall never be reconciled. His last angry words to me, "*If you go I'll never call you 'Mum' again,*" will re-echo in my mind forever.

My own on-going recovery has taken three years, the length of time we have been apart. It has been partially effective because of the insight I gained both into Parental Alienation Syndrome and a better understanding of the tensions arising in my past life both as a parent and as a wife.

What has helped equally is the harsh honesty with which I interrogated myself, and questioned the wisdom of the sudden abrupt manner in which I left the marital home. Friends and family tried to help but only we can finally help ourselves. At first, however, the brutality with which all ties were instantly cut almost crushed me into suicide.

This book is also dedicated to two women in very unhappy marriages who did take their own lives, in one friend's case after her four children (mid to late twenties) had persuaded her to continue working at her 30-year old marriage.

My own marriage as it turned out lasted 25 years too long and should never have taken place at all.

If you do decide to end your marriage or leave home without your children even for the most noble or selfish of reasons, or decide to put your children into care for reasons of temporary ill-health or to escape from a violent home life, and without having fully prepared either yourself, your spouse/partner or your children, be warned. The following months and years might turn out to be an emotional test of epic proportions for all the family, but most of all for you and your relationships with your children.

You as the parent who has left children behind or given them away into care might find yourself under scrutiny and will have to undergo an examination so rigorous it would bring most people to their knees. It will not, in truth, be a fair trial. In most cases, your estranged partner or your children will have appointed themselves judge and jury before you open your mouth or pick up a pen to defend yourself. Their verdict, a foregone conclusion in their eyes, is you have been a failure as a parent because you apparently abandoned them. Learn from my mistakes.

This is not an anti-marriage book or an anti-relationship book although some critics may see it as such. I, like many other parents who have experienced painfully unsuccessful relationships, would like to see the entire process of becoming married re-evaluated. It should be made much more difficult to marry to increase the dignity and status of marriage in our society, underpinning its unquestionable value as a permanent, stable and loving long-term environment in which two people nurture children wisely. I should like divorce to be made much easier as long as parents and legal practitioners protect the children of divorce from becoming mentally abused in high-conflict family-split scenarios.

Everyone, particularly the young, whether they intend marrying or whether they intend living together, should be encouraged to seek advice before agreeing to share their life with someone who may only be known as a romantic partner but with whom they may at some point intend to have a child. Education courses such as those run by Marriage Care could be a start. Marriage Care *"design and manage marriage preparation courses around the country. Operating from a parish base, multi-disciplinary teams work in, and for, the local community. They encourage couples to explore, test and, in some cases, renew their commitment to marriage. These courses, running for 6-8 hours, focus on commitment, communication and the management of conflict as the basis for forming loving, lasting relationships."*

This book could also be described as a damage-limitation guide on the best way to end a marriage or relationship, and a guide to protect children's continuing and future relationships with both parents.

It also stands as a warning to those parents who may be having an affair or suffering ill-health or seeking a brief 'breathing space' in their marriage or relationship through a temporary separation. They may be naively unaware of how the vacuum, however short-lived, left by their absence in the family home could be irrevocably manipulated by an aggrieved parent and thereby damage a child's relationship with the other parent for the rest of their lives.

I also want to discuss Parental Alienation Syndrome, to make it more widely known in the United Kingdom's medical, legal and judicial system through debate and discussion. Peggie Ward of PACE believes that in recognising that alienation has taken place,

"the courts must look to the long term best interests of the child in terms of custody because the alienation progress will continue. Courts must act decisively and explicitly in cases of high conflict divorce and alienation. Orders must be pragmatic and the grounds for decisions must be explained in terms that make it less likely that one party can claim a moral victory and the other feel shame of defeat. Courts must use their knowledge and power to understand the family system, to recognise high conflict alienation cases, and to make appropriate, timely and specific referrals and recommendations. By recognising alienation in its early forms, prevention of future harm to the child and family may well be possible. Intervention, at any point along the continuum of harm, is crucial to prevent further harm."

And so say all of us. Using the Child Support Agency's current figures [October 1999] – and these are only drawn, they stress, from the people who use their agency – I am told that there are 812,000 fathers and 51,900 mothers living apart from their children in the United Kingdom today. Behind those figures, there will be a huge range of circumstances and a wide variety of contact arrangements, although some parents like me will have no contact at all.

Some parents, particularly mothers, might have thought as I did that they were the only ones in the world who had left home without their children. A few have had to take a gut-wrenching decision in the most tragic of circumstances to put children into care to protect them from physical or emotional abuse.They have now become alienated from them.

Some of those parents living apart from their children probably wanted to die at some point as I did when they realised they would never see their children again. Some chronically and morbidly dejected parents have unhappily taken their own lives. Some have taken the lives of their children as well when their marriages or relationships broke up.

I did things all the wrong way, but I hope this guide together with legal and emotional guidance separating parents should seek from professional agencies and counsellors will help them come to a decision which is fundamentally right for all the family.

It needs much more than luck or chance when parents seek to make a new life for themselves in life-changing circumstances because they are also destroying a child's family, a child who has no say in the matter at all.

If you are thinking of leaving your home, your spouse and your children – even temporarily – I hope you think long and hard on the best way to do it to achieve minimum pain for the whole family but particularly for your children.

Public perception of splitting up a family and archaic views regarding "ownership" of children has to change for our children's sake. Divorce, like marriage, can sometimes be an unexpectedly positive and eventually enriching experience for the two people involved but seldom for children unless they are properly prepared, guided and supported throughout. Some people emerge from marriage break-up more mature and able to handle whatever life throws at them. But children must come first.

In June 1998, nearly two years after I had left, and shortly after the death of my eldest son, I read an article in a tabloid newspaper which moved me to write to the person concerned. It was the story of a 38-year-old woman who had left her husband and sons, 10 and 15. "*Why I don't regret abandoning my boys*" was the banner headline followed by a minor headline: "*I don't feel I love my sons because I no longer know them*." Her husband had turned the children against her. All had become strangers to each other.

Through the reporter, I wrote sympathetically to this mother, outlining my own circumstances and was persuaded by the tabloid to be interviewed for, what I believed, would be a follow-up type story.

I was foolishly naive. The story they printed was heavily biased towards the 'tripe and titillation' human-interest aspect. But I did receive a number of letters from mothers in similar situations offering me support, compassion and their own harrowing stories of separation from their children.

We all expressed huge relief at our discovery that we were not alone in suffering on-going agony by being separated after divorce from children who had turned against us. Perhaps, too, Parental Alienation Syndrome was eagerly seized on and readily identifiable by some of us to partly explain our children's behaviour which had a common pattern for us all. We found mutual and indescribable help in sharing our stories.

Their stories stand as a stark warning to those parents thinking of leaving partners, perhaps leaving children in the family home, or those parents thinking of putting children into care, even if they believe it is in children's best interests.

I can only write as a mother and have included mainly mother's stories for two reasons: firstly, I believe it is mothers, in many cases, who suffer the most in being apart and alienated from children. In most 'normal', natural mothers there is a fundamental cherishing, nurturing instinct vested in them: we delivered our children and have been in most cases, principal carers from birth, 24 hours a day for many years. Secondly, few fathers wanted to write their stories.

Who, though, can measure which parent hurts the most when alienated from precious children? I acknowledge wholeheartedly that there are probably more fathers than mothers living apart or alienated from their children. Most care just as deeply as a mother, some even more, and many have suffered immeasurably. However, I can only write as a mother.

Once a mother, always a mother. I have heard it said – time and time again – mothers are not people. Even if children, of whatever age, neglect, abuse, ignore, love or hate their mothers, these mothers must always remain in the family home. Regardless of their reasons for leaving, whether for another man or simply to make a life of their own away from a love-less or violent marriage, a mother's past life and future useful life as such, is extinguished without warning if she leaves home without her children. Children expect both parents, but particularly a mother, to have few rights except those of promoting their children's interests within the family unit and to do so unquestioningly throughout their lives.

This is what most caring parents want above all else but why can't they do so outside of their own marriage and with the whole-hearted support of the other parent?

If one parent does go, leaving children behind, it seems some relinquish all claims to a share in those children's lives. They are punished in cold blood, without warning, and with hard-hearted vengeance. Some parents, particularly mothers, must not expect the right to direct their own lives as individuals whatever the ages of their children. Even if some wait to leave their marriage until the children are older, those children perhaps even married or leading independent lives themselves, it seems to make no difference. A muddled jumble of ugly emotions rears up: jealousy, possessiveness, betrayal, unforgiving anger.

Children feel very badly let down if one parent leaves, or if one of them decides to put them into care, whatever the circumstances, and are unable to separate feelings for a parent who has nurtured and cared for them unselfishly, from those feelings for that parent as an individual with needs. They feel unable to forgive and have no remorse about punishing that parent.

Some younger children are aided by the other parent into believing the situation is all black or all white: one parent is all-bad, the other is all-good. With the immaturity of childhood and being susceptible to emotional abuse, younger children are not given freedom to view their departing or absent parent sympathetically.

But even some young adult children seem indiscriminate, unable to judge their parent as a separate person or as an individual who has chosen to live a different life outside the marriage. In their eyes, parents are selfish to want a life of their own even if they have an unblemished track record of having devoted themselves loyally and constantly, sometimes for decades, to family life as well as to a failed marriage.

Parents only exist, in the eyes of some children, to serve the emotional and physical demands of the family unit, to remain forever an unchanging part of the children's own changing circumstances, serving as a life support system for children, just in case it is needed sometime.

That devotion can sometimes become a life sentence for some mothers with no life outside the home, who may be suicidally unhappy in their marriage and who should be sympathetically viewed as victims needing support or release from a prison sentence but who are invariably perceived as villains.

Patricia Bailey of MATCH (Mothers Apart from Their Children) writes:

"Contrary to popular belief, mothers who take the decision to live apart from their children almost always have their children's best interests at heart. Not all, though, have had the chance to share in decisions about their children's future. Many have had to give up custody against their will and through no fault of their own. Reasons include poverty, illness, fear for safety and sometimes, sheer ignorance of the workings of the legal system. Women who live apart from their children are looked upon with more suspicion than men in the same situation. All their stories are very different but some examples are:

- Social Services took the child away because they didn't think the mother could cope with the child's handicap.

- When the marriage broke down, the father had the support of his family to look after the children. The mother didn't and so thought they would be better off with him.

- The mother was ill so agreed the child should live with the father. When he died, the court gave custody to the step-mother even though their mother was well again."

Sometimes parents are apart from children if a marriage to a foreign national has ended and the children are abducted. These separations can last many years, sometimes as much as ten or more. An example might be:

- The children did not return from a holiday visit to another country with the parent who abducted them. After many years being naturalised in that parent's country, they sometimes choose to remain.

When you read this book, imagine you are hearing many voices: those of parents who have lost children and have become so traumatised by injustice both in their own homes and later in the courts or so defeated by the loss of their children they cannot even begin to express a small measure of their sorrow or anger. These parents have lost their voices and have sunk down into a dark pit of depression which has closed over their heads, shutting out the world, leaving them in an inner world of despair where life without beloved children seems barren and meaningless.

It is thought there are now over 150,000 mothers living apart from their children in the United Kingdom and the numbers are rising. Some became alienated from their children in circumstances they believed were unique to themselves and that they were the only mothers whose children could not or did not want to live with them and had turned against them.

Many parents in re-building their new lives without children, continue to keep quiet about their existence because it is too painful to mention them or because there is too much explaining as to why their children are not living with them. Many dread questions from new people, *"Do you have any children?"* or *"How many children do you have?"* This latter question is difficult when the parent may be in a new relationship with new children but does not have contact with children from the previous relationship. On the one hand she/he does not want to deny their existence. On the other, if an honest answer is given, too many questions or judgements may be made when one is trying to re-build a new life.

Few people know about my children in the place where I live now. Explanations can sometimes seem like excuses. Silence is better and much less painful.

Penny Cross
May 2000

EMOTIONAL ABUSE: THE BEGINNING

"The Sudden Abandonment: the second type of couple likely to reach an impasse at the interactional level are those whose marriages fall apart suddenly, without warning. One partner may have a love affair and leave abruptly, one spouse may flee from what he or she perceives as danger or emotional abuse. The salient characteristics of these situations is their lack of an opportunity for closure, for a chance to talk it through, to hear and attempt to understand the causes of the separation. Instead, what remains is an enormous sense of betrayal. The abandoned spouse feels hurt and angry, totally focused on the deceit of the other person. Humiliation and rage make it extremely difficult to deal with the separation and begin the healing process so necessary for post-divorce adjustment."

Caught in the middle: Protecting the children of high-conflict divorce
Carla B. Garrity, Mitchell A. Baris, 1997

About six months after leaving my husband, I ran into an ex-neighbour in a department store:

"How are you?", she asked.

"I'm all right but I miss the children dreadfully."

"Well, you should have thought of that before then, shouldn't you?"

I looked at her blankly, stunned by her reaction, stung by the unsaid ugly judgement she had just made, and walked away. Did she really think I had wanted to leave them at home? Did she honestly believe I had made a choice, that they were perhaps a nuisance, that I no longer cared enough for them and wanted to leave them behind? What morally principled and caring parent would or could think that cherished children would be left behind through choice? I had left my husband, not my children, because I had no home and no money to take them with me. Did she not understand how much I ached for their smell, their touch, their noise, their voices? Daily life, now without them, was a living bereavement, a one-day-at-a-time existence, putting one foot in front of the other in a meaningless pretence of trying to find a way and reasons to move forward.

This cruel judgement, in which one mother had tried and sentenced me, in that one sentence, was to be repeated many times by others. Her judgement, as I was to discover later, mattered little. I was to judge myself even more harshly many times afterwards and to acknowledge that the sentencing, a lifetime's punishment of alienation by my children, might be a just one in some instances.

***

In July 1996 I walked out of my job one morning during an exceptionally busy period. My doctor diagnosed acute stress. One week later I walked out of my 23 year marriage at three in the morning leaving my husband, my 12 year old twins at home in bed and my 20 year old eldest son at home after an angry exchange of words with both he and with my husband. My 18 year old son was living a few miles away in his own flat.

The next time I saw my children, except for a week spent with them shortly after I left home was at an inquest two years later in July 1998 into the death of my eldest son. My three remaining children, my second eldest son now 20 and son and daughter twins now 14, sat closely together hemmed in on both sides by young friends. Their father was not present. All ignored me through the entire hour it took the coroner to pronounce a verdict on my dead son. To onlookers, we might have been complete strangers.

I had walked out of my marriage abruptly in July 1996 to end it. In my own mind it had ended many years ago. In my children's minds, however, it ended at three o'clock one morning when I left them in bed.

Knowing I had to find another home soon for my younger children, I equally knew they would be better off at home, for the moment, in familiar surroundings, near their school and friends, while I got myself better, stronger and able to cope.

Not knowing what was going to happen immediately, because my mind was in turmoil, I was confident I would soon make another home for my two younger children, where they could spend part of their time there, and that it would probably be with someone for whom I had come to care deeply in recent months. This man, someone we, as a family, had befriended following the recent death of his wife, was twenty years older than I. Our friendship had soon turned to love.

Within hours of my leaving home, my estranged husband's disturbed, extreme nature, his hysterical, highly emotional response to the ending of our marriage, resulted in his threatening several times, in front of the children, to commit suicide. Telephoning me daily, he included spite, threats, appeals or all three in conversations which sometimes lasted 20-45 minutes, starting on that first day, 23 July, with only a half-hour break in-between.

"I hope you won't mind my saying this but the house is so much nicer without you. I promise I'll change, I know all my worst faults, just please come home. Have a rest and then come home."

Determined not to give him false hope, I made this clear in every conversation.

Sometimes he hinted at "topping himself". Worried sick, particularly if the children should come home from school and find he had done so, as had happened to the niece of a friend, I telephoned our doctor who lived nearby. He rang that evening to say my husband was very distressed, continually crying and having enormous difficulty in coming to terms with the ending of his marriage.

On that first day after I left, I had telephoned the children several times. Sometimes I was allowed to speak to them but not always.

"They're too upset to speak to you. You don't know what you've done".

I tried to be honest, positive, sensitive, understanding with the children, when I was allowed to speak to them, but did not offer hope the marriage could be mended. Sometimes they were tearful: I said they were to imagine my arms were tightly around them and that I well understood their father was very upset but I would like to have a long talk with them. Would they would like to come and stay with me the following week (the beginning of the summer holidays) at my stepfather's and we could have time together? They agreed.

I asked my daughter to speak to other friends who had divorced parents (I knew there were several, one quite recently). She said she had already spoken with Katherine (who lived with her father) who had told her,

"Whatever happens, remember it's not your fault. And at Christmas time and birthdays, you'll get two big presents."

I agreed this was quite true. It had happened in my own life, my own parents having separated while I was a teenager.

I asked their father if they could come and stay with me the following week. He agreed they could be collected on Friday morning. He asked to speak to me when I did arrive but I felt there was nothing to say, not wanting to prolong emotional scenes I knew instinctively would be played out. The children seemed slightly subdued but happy to see me, giving hugs and kisses.

For the first time I can remember my daughter reached up to kiss her father's cheek and he did not recoil, as he always had before, in typically mocking humorous disgust. They hugged each other – again, something I had never, ever witnessed.

When we got back to my step-father's home, I made it clear they were welcome to ring their father at any time, knowing he would appreciate it, being very distressed. I encouraged them to have private conversations on the telephone in the bedroom if they wished. Discussing our feelings through the day, and in bed at night (we all three shared a room), we had honest conversations about the marriage, my changing outlook and my understanding of their own thoughts. I did not criticise their father except to say I had lived with him for 23 years and could no longer continue with the marriage, needing to begin a new life for myself.

At all times we were loving towards each other and their affection was spontaneous, warm and always there.

That week the children continued to telephone their father, he continued to telephone me, to cry, to abuse, to threaten, to plead. I held firm, making an appointment to see solicitors for legal advice.

Very early one morning a few days later, the Ward Sister of the Cardiac Unit at the local hospital near the family home telephoned to say my husband had asked her to ring me to say he was in hospital. She did not sound very worried: "Just in for overnight observation, admitted with chest pains – ring about 11.00 am to see what the duty doctor says but he's probably going to be discharged." I did not tell the children until I was in full possession of all the facts from our family doctor who later rang back to say he, himself, had discovered it had been an anxiety attack, nothing more. I did not trouble to ring the hospital but told the children to ring their father to cheer him up.

Horrified to find them in tears, I found he had told them he had had a heart attack. Enraged, I angrily accused him of self-inflicting the anxiety attack as a cheap sympathy bid and, further, blowing it up into a full-scale heart attack. I was reminded of his lying on the rugby field years previously, faking injury while gaining extra time and boasting of it afterwards.

This scenario, combined with my sudden departure, so affected my children they seemed to have to deal with one shock after another. Is it any wonder they have never forgiven me for abandoning their father and later they accused me of abandoning them.

The malice escalated on a horrifying scale after he found out a few days later, quite by chance, about the new man in my life, who was not only a near neighbour and a man he had befriended but was also twenty years older than he was.

Now he refused to let me speak or see them, saying "it would upset them." My eldest son put the telephone down as soon as he heard my voice. All five put their opinions of me, using abusive and foul language, in a letter – no envelope – together with a photograph of this man, thrusting it into the hands of friends in supermarkets, posting it through letterboxes of friends far and wide, hiring a car to race up and down the country to put his side of the story, denouncing me as a prostitute. No one was spared an embellished exaggeration of the story, including elderly spinster aunts overseas.

A letter attacking me and my new partner ("the old man") in scathing terms, printed by the printing unit at the college where I worked, contained abominable messages.

"lots of hate from your daughter (in case you didn't know)" and "thanks for neglecting us, many farts. PS we've changed the locks for your benefit" from my youngest son.

My eldest son wrote, "I don't even miss you. You're gone and our house is happy now." In conversation with my friends and family, he frequently referred to me as a prostitute.

In-between my leaving home and becoming part of the legal system, past history as a mother was re-written. In interviews with the Divorce Court Welfare Officer my ex-husband stated a

"tense and unhappy atmosphere existed caused by her volatile temper, her unrealistic demands of the children concerning their schoolwork and her extreme irritability over routine matters in the household".

My two older sons stated:

"as a result of numerous incidents, occurring from when they were approximately 10 years old, they have decided they want no further contact with their mother."

I vividly recall my mothering life at that time. The boys were 8 and 10. The twins were 2.

My widowed mother-in-law in her sixties was mentally and physically exhausted, having nursed my father-in-law for 8 years until his death after he had been brain-damaged following a routine hernia operation. She had been further traumatised after her husband's death when her step-son and his family of four teenagers, living with her for a year after his death, left after a blazing row, stealing all her possessions and furniture, leaving just a bed, a chair and a few other things.

As always over the years, she had absolutely no one but me to take an interest or offer practical help. Now she wanted telephone support, frequent visiting, re-furnishing of her house. Within a few months she developed eccentricities, noticed only by me. I followed this up and had her diagnosed. She had Alzheimer's Disease.

She worsened rapidly, exhibiting a bizarre pattern of aggressive behaviour and was for the next three years a drain on my physical and mental energies. She was by then telephoning several times a day, and the police telephoned me at least once a week. Neighbours reported that she frequently answered the door naked except for several brassieres, threw saucepans of boiling water on passers by and locked herself out of the house repeatedly.

I visited her frequently, kept up a barrage of pressure on Social Services, her GP and the consultant psychogeriatrician to have her sectioned under the Mental Health Act. They all argued that they were morally and legally obliged to wait until she was "bad" enough and a danger both to herself as well as to others before she could be sectioned.

My husband took no active part in supporting me or his mother. He was sacked from a nationally known project for "an attitude problem", later being offered a job 150 miles away.

We moved, took turns to keep up a week-end 240-mile round trip for four months to visit his mother, moving her to a nursing home near us and, finally, a psychiatric home, a few miles away. I kept up twice-weekly visits, my husband going just once, his two brothers and family not at all. She died after a few months following a major epileptic fit.

My husband had a job for six months after her death and was then made redundant. My twins were then under 10, the older children young teenagers. I had a series of part-time temping jobs, sometimes walking quickly across the city from the morning job to the afternoon one.

My older sons had educational or behavioural problems at school, frequently clashed with teachers in their hostility towards authority, my second eldest later being excluded from school for one week for vandalism. I was deeply worried about this son's progress at school, having moved him from one junior school to another to see if another environment would improve his attitude. It worked for a while but then we moved.

At his third junior school his teacher called him, as previous teachers had, "the laziest pupil I've ever had in 30 years of teaching". I refused to believe this of my bright, fast-talking, quick-thinking son, insisted that he be tested by an educational psychologist who found, after testing, he had a dysgraphia problem.

"Difficulties with writing often leads to major misunderstandings by teachers and parents, and consequently, to many frustrations for the student. This is especially true for the bright, linguistically fast student who encounters a major stumbling block when dealing with written expression due to the lack of smooth, efficient automaticity in letter and word formation. These students struggle to translate their thoughts and knowledge, which then denies their teachers the opportunity to understand what they know. An astute teacher or parent may suspect dysgraphia in a student by observing writing performances. All too often, however, the student's performance is interpreted as poor motivation, carelessness, laziness, or excessive speed. " (http://dyslexia-ca.org/dysgraph.htm)

My daughter, at 9 years old at her junior school, was cautioned to "curb her aggressive nature", according to one school report. (Now, at 15, this aggression continues as I'm told, recently, she has now been banned by her high school from playing for their school team after threatening a member of a visiting team.)

It was against this background, during two decades of deepening economic gloom, witnessing their father's unsuccessful search for employment after a sacking and a redundancy, worried sick about my older sons' future and their negative attitudes at school, that they remember me as "harsh and unfair".

They are probably right.

In conversations with the Divorce Court Welfare Officer which he initiated, my eldest son was

> "particularly keen to describe the depth of his negative feelings towards his mother. However, [my second eldest son]'s feelings towards her appear to be equally as strong."

My eldest son further stated:

> "his mother always appears reasonable to outsiders but within the home her behaviour towards all four children has been very hostile and destructive."

The younger children's memories were, she continued

"of their mother's harsh and unfair disciplining of them and the way in which she generated a bad atmosphere in the house by her criticism of them."

They talked about

"wanting to divorce their mother and asked if there were any legal steps they could take to prevent their mother, or the Court, from forcing them to have contact."

They said they

"have difficulty in remembering any positive aspects of their relationship with their mother.

Recent events, e.g. birthday parties

"were dismissed as occurring when they were younger."

Quite, quite, quite untrue.

Clues to partly understanding my children's rejection may lie in my former husband's personality together with his strong need for status and prominence.

In losing me to a man twenty years older, he thought he was in danger of looking foolish. In the past, whenever a situation occurred where he might lose public esteem, he had re-written his role in the situation to emerge understandably with some dignity, but the extreme nature of his reactions confirm a pattern believed to encompass paranoia, suggesting a disturbed psychological temperament. My ex-husband saw himself as powerful, never impotent. A nonconforming individualist, he would be disappointed to learn that in his reactions he was being absolutely conventional in conforming to a pattern which Dr. Gardner has seen many times and has documented as "The Fury of the Scorned Man" described in the chapter entitled Clinical Manifestations in the Alienating Parent in The Parental Alienation Syndrome:

"...There are sources of anger other than financial privation, and loss of self-esteem is one of them. A man in such a situation may wish to wreak vengeance upon a woman who has rejected him; taking away her children will predictably be the most effective way of achieving this goal.

...Just as a woman is likely to be angry if her husband has a new involvement, a man is likely to be angry if his wife has a new involvement, especially if the new involvement ante-dated and was the cause of the separation."

To minimise this new and above all public hurt, he needed to inflict greater hurt on me. The one thing which I valued, above all else, was my children and my strong, driving need to give them as stable, secure and as happy a childhood as was possible. Knowing this, he actively project-managed a programme to annihilate the children's memories of me as a caring mother. He needed to mask the influence he exerted over the children, making them believe "a catalogue of abuse and neglect of them" are true memories.

Such was his ingenuity that his effect was barely discernible.

He encouraged the children to remember every occasion when I had disciplined them, highlighting these, discouraging or obliterating memories of the genuinely happy times.

After I left letters, birthday, Christmas cards and presents from me were returned to my solicitor with hand-written notes from my 12 year old twins.

"We do not wish to hear from your client."

I no longer send them cards or gifts because I feel they do not want a continual reminder that I want them in my life. They have sent me clear messages that I am no longer a 'wanted' person in their lives and it would be upsetting for them if I continued to press home my own needs at the expense of theirs. If they need to refer to me nowadays, as in occasional legal correspondence, no name is used.

When I think of the times I used to call out in frustration, "Just let me be for five minutes without someone calling out 'Mum!', I am very sad. No one will ever call me by that name again.

THE DEATH OF A RELATIONSHIP

"...Uncertainty, aggression and a lack of concentration tend to develop in children whose parents quarrel and fight on a regular basis. In general, the expression of anger between people is one of the most disturbing and difficult experiences which children have to handle. It can produce some of the most problematic social behaviour.

Overt conflict between parents in the form of shouting, swearing, threatening to walk out and throwing things at each other is likely to cause children both emotional and behavioural problems."

Attachment Theory for Social Work Practice,
David Howe, School of Health and Social Work,
University of East Anglia, Norwich.

If we are in an unhappy relationship whether married or not, filing cabinets could probably be filled with the reasons why it has been breaking down over many years or shows the signs of being about to break down. The original reasons we married or decided to live together are sometimes long forgotten, quite unrelated to why we try to remain together. Financially strained situations, shared possessions, a joint home, but most of all children, contribute to the reasons why poor relationships last or married people stay together after love, affection or respect has dried up and disappeared. Children are the glue in sticking together a poor relationship.

In Relate's Guide to Better Relationships, Sarah Litvinoff describes 'liking' someone as the 'backbone of love'. She asks:

"How much do you actually like your partner? Like can seem a rather weedy emotion compared to love but it is one of the most important components in making your relationship last. It might seem surprising but some people fall in love and form relationships with partners they don't like very much. If you enjoy each other's company, find each other interesting as human beings, approve of the way each other thinks and behaves, you stand a good chance of feeling the same once the 'in love'

feelings have passed. If there are things that irritate or bore you about your partner, or of which you disapprove, or which make you feel cross or contemptuous, these will matter to you more once you have stopped feeling madly in love. A question to ask yourself is, 'Would I want to be friends with this person if we weren't in love?'"

It has been bitter and painful for those parents who have contributed their stories to re-live the experiences of unhappy marriages or partnerships by writing them out again for this book, and we can only imagine the initial and prolonged suffering of their children left behind in the family home. "Children are very resilient", we are told, "they bounce back soon particularly if they're very young."

Do they? Why do so many, many adults, left as young children, still remember every detail of their parents' parting or divorce with pain? Why do so many, left as young adults, never forget or forgive? Children, unless they are babies or toddlers, will remember everything with absolute clarity.

In his book, Breaking up without cracking up: Reducing the pain of separation and divorce, Christopher Compston discusses the personal effect of divorce on him first as a child, and later as a husband as well as much later professionally. Having had considerable experience of divorce as both a barrister and a judge and been involved in hundreds of divorce cases, he says that "In one month I might handle 30 to 40 divorces, sometimes more:"

"I was 12 when my parents divorced and I can vividly remember the unhappiness of that time, not least my father's absence, my mother's bitterness and the constant lack of money. Years later, these wounds have almost healed but some scar tissue remains.

Thus, both personally and professionally, I have some experience and, although we are all unique, certain patterns of behaviour and misbehaviour emerge."

In The Family through Divorce: How you can limit the damage, Janet Reibstein, PhD and Roger Bamber have written a guide to the legal and emotional issues and describe it as a book "for the whole family because divorce is a whole-family process". They believe that:

"It can take anything from three to five years to recover from divorce-generated upheaval. In addition, latent influences of the divorce process can appear many years later when the child reaches a vulnerable stage of development such as adolescence. This is seen particularly in the fact that children whose parents have divorced form their own sexual relationships earlier on, marry earlier, have a higher than average incidence of divorce themselves, achieve lower than expectable school performances and leave school earlier."

You may not be dissuaded from leaving but I have written this book to persuade you to think more deeply about the manner of your going, what you say to your spouse or partner as well as to your children, and to urge you to consider how to make it less painful for them, and ultimately for all of you and your future relationships.

Giving examples of how different families managed to involve their children either negatively or positively in the divorce process, Janet Reibstein and Roger Bamber emphasise that it is our children, the children of divorced parents, who will be the next generation responsible for attitudes towards family life:

"If the process of restructuring the family is to stand any chance of success, the needs of children involved especially have to be understood and accommodated. They are almost always unwilling participants in marital separation and divorce. If children can be eased through the process then the chances for the family as a whole to emerge successfully are greatly enhanced."

In the shocking heartache of discovering that your spouse or partner wants to end your marriage or relationship, or in the excitement of having a serious affair or beginning a new long-term relationship, people are sometimes carelessly unthinking, deliberately inconsiderate or just plain selfish. One thought may be uppermost: how to get out of the old relationship and into the new one as quickly as possible.

For the partner who is left behind, another thought may be uppermost: how to be as vindictive as possible using the children as weapons.

As we had discussed divorce and separation many, many times after heated arguments during our 25 year marriage, and as I had found it very difficult to talk to someone who was extremely eloquent, fluent with excuses, smooth-talking with promises, I felt in my own situation that more talking would be useless and a waste of my energy. With the hard-won experience I now have I can state most emphatically and categorically that I was quite wrong.

It did not once occur to me to consider what an immensely powerful effect a sudden walking out would have on the balance of my husband's mind. I had always wanted to equal his verbal skills or argument-winning. I wanted to do something without words to achieve the effect of a barrier coming down on his eloquence.

Had I been in a calmer frame of mind, perhaps having consulted self-help books or professionals for advice and support, or been carefully plotting to walk out on my marriage at a certain time or a certain day, I would still have gone for a divorce but things might have turned out quite differently with careful planning and preparation.

Ritual and custom are important processes of our life whether in the most impoverished or wealthiest of families. Society recognises the importance of publicly welcoming in a new life or ushering out the old which is why we place such importance on the ceremonies of marriages, funerals or baptisms to distinguish these family-based occasions. I should have anticipated there needed some kind of formal conduct or protocol to mark and finalise my old life before beginning the new one.

Such formality should probably have included much preparation of the children, myself, my situation, as well as perhaps most importantly, a face-to-face discussion with my former husband. We do not have in our society any occasion as yet to mark the important family event of divorce or splitting up. Perhaps it is time someone had the courage to initiate these because most people going through a divorce, or the process of splitting up a family, know instinctively this is a momentous family occasion, perhaps even more than the traditional positive ones which are marked with much ceremony.

I knew I could not stand up to my husband's emotional pressure or possibly physical threats, knowing intuitively there would be a risk of violence too towards the person who was potentially to be my partner in my new life. Perhaps I should have arranged for a friend to be on hand to support him. Would this have helped? I don't know. It might have been appalling for me, dreadful for my husband but kinder for him as I was initiating the break-up. There is no easy way to think about the right way, or an acceptable form of words to use, in preparing to pass on a painful message which you know is not going to be well received.

Passing on bad news is something no one wants to do. There's no comfortable way. You know there will be disbelief, a refusal to accept it, maybe even rage, anger and violence. Perhaps I wanted to avoid even more argument or longer discussion, knowing I couldn't cope in my own weakened emotional state. It is human nature for the one who is going to be badly hurt to demand a full explanation, to need time to make sense of it, to go over and over the reasons.

With Dignity[6], a support group for people whose partners or spouses have left or divorced them, have the following advice for those who are forced to come to terms with life without their partner. With Dignity is the first organisation of its kind in the UK. Their primary aims are to

"help, support and befriend people confronted with suspected or confirmed adultery of their partner or those still coming to terms with the loss of their partner through divorce.

First of all it is the acceptance that he/she has gone from your life and will not be coming back which is the hardest thing to bear. You cannot and will not accept this for quite some time. It is so painful, the pain is so hard to describe but it's like a big black cloak has wrapped itself around you and swallowed you. The pain is larger than life. Every day seems the same. You go through the motions of the day, evening and night but the emptiness and pain is still there.

When your partner has left you for someone else you will experience shock (bereavement), acceptance, anger, vengeance, loneliness, emptiness, guilt, grief. It is like you have built a house of love, brick by brick. Emotions, plans, happiness, blood, sweat and tears, your future, your life together. You have put everything into it to make it strong, secure and safe...Your whole world comes crashing down around you until there is nothing left, just devastation, trauma and shock. The hurt, pain and confusion is larger than life.

Coming to terms with your loss is called letting go. Letting go of the one you have loved, letting go of the marriage, letting go of the life you once shared, and this does take time."

With Dignity recognises that a broken marriage can be almost impossibly difficult for the aggrieved partner to cope with alone and that he/she will be in acute need of real support and specialist advice for some time to come.

Another organisation supporting divorcees, Divorce Recovery Workshop believes that the loss of a spouse is one of the most devastating traumas anyone can ever experience, and that in a marriage break-up the individual usually experiences all the shock of a bereaved person plus even more conflicting emotions.

It has been running a workshop offering a secure environment for discussion and understanding of feelings twice a year in the Maidenhead area since 1992 with 30 to 60 attendees. The course consists of six weekly evening sessions to helps the individual come to terms with a relationship that has irretrievably broken down. A residential weekend in Devon attracted 74. DRW believe that:

"Divorce results in the death of a marriage but does not have the finality of a physical death. The vestiges of a former way of life remain to remind and overshadow a present existence. It's a hurt that goes deep and is accompanied by the doubt that it will ever heal."

On their website, they promote themselves as

"a UK nationwide self-help group run by volunteers who have attended the workshop. There are no 'experts' but all those present will have personally experienced a relationship break-up. The depth of emotional suffering of the newly separated or divorced is not generally realised. While society allows the bereaved years to adjust, the divorced are frequently expected to 'pull themselves together' in a matter of weeks, unaided.

The workshop enables people to better understand what they are going through, provides them with support from others in the same situation and assists in the process of readjustment in their lives."

It is critically important if you are the one initiating the break-up or even if you are just thinking about leaving your partner that you recognise, openly and honestly, the injury you will undoubtedly be doing to his/her emotional health and mental well-being as well as the potentially harmful, long-term side effects your children may suffer as a consequence. Unless you are all well prepared, the groundwork could soon be ready for a set of circumstances to arise in which Parental Alienation Syndrome or variations on it may flourish and prosper to damage you and your children forever.

Tony Gough, in his book, Couples Parting, recognises the importance of acknowledging that the ending of a relationship is like experiencing a death but that the theme of dealing with or discussing death itself is a subject which our culture or society usually avoids or side-steps. Hanging on to a relationship which is dead or dying merely prolongs the inevitable agony when bereavement-like symptoms will be experienced later. He feels this highlights society's widespread avoidance of the subject of death and bereavement:

"We must not expect it to be otherwise when considering the ending of an important relationship. That, too, involves a kind of 'death' experience in terms of its finality and its unwelcome nature. In my opinion, it is not death that is at fault but our inadequate and often immature reactions to it. We have all become experts at avoiding the painfully obvious merely because in admitting it we shall have to deal with it. Having owned it, we must take responsibility for it. Rather than do this, we choose to go on denying it.

...After the breaking down of the relationship we need to come to terms with the 'breaking out' of the old patterns associated with that previous relationship. Since such patterns of intimacy and togetherness may have been built up over many years (my first marriage lasted over twenty-five years) there is no way in which they are going to disappear suddenly. This is precisely the problem we face when a partner dies: how do we 'uncouple' and become single again."

If you are quite serious about ending your marriage or partnership, take one step at a time as *gradually* as you can and remember that you are sounding the death knell for an important relationship in which many people in your family, particularly the children, have a vested interest.

Just recently I heard of a mother who had walked out of her 12-year marriage giving her children (11 and 8) and her husband 24 hours notice. She had already been to see a solicitor, set up a flat with her new love (who had left his wife and children, 8 and 6). Two days later she invited her daughter, 11, to (a) meet her new stepfather-to-be and (b) inspect, what was to be, the daughter's bedroom in the new flat. All in the space of two days.

Another woman of my acquaintance left her husband over a year ago after 27 years in, what had been for the last 17 years, a loveless marriage. She had fallen in love with someone the family had known for some time and her love was returned. Her three children, daughters of 22 and 25 and a son of 17 had condemned her for leaving their father, calling her a whore and a slut. Her husband had sworn at her in front of her children, using the most vulgar, profane and coarse abuse. She had been a devoted mother, a wife of great respectability, had never looked at another man in 27 years until now, and, despite wanting to leave the marriage many, many years before, had wanted to wait until her daughters had completed university and her son was grown-up. They have now cut her out of their lives.

You may think you have given out all the signals over a period of months or years that you are the end of your tether, you are thinking of leaving or you want to end your marriage but how absolutely clear are these signs to your spouse and children?

Look at the situation through their eyes whatever the ages of your own children, and regardless of whether they are young children or young adults. Try to imagine their shock if you give them less notice than the time it takes a second-class letter to reach its destination that their family world has not only come to an end but has in fact died. Imagine the impact similar news might have on you.

If you are just thinking about leaving or are serious about leaving and if you have children of any age, is there any way you could think about the right way to prepare your husband/wife/partner and children for the ending of your marriage or relationship?

Is there any advice you could get from professionals, advice agencies, the church or other self-help books which would help you? It is worth thinking about extensively and it is worth researching long and hard. It will, hopefully, repay all your efforts in the end if you consider the right way, the right time as well as the right words to tell your family you believe your marriage or partnership is coming to an end in the very near future.

If you value the continued relationship between you and your children, if you want to keep future contact with your spouse or partner as amicable as possible for the sake of your children, do nothing for the moment. Do absolutely nothing until you are quite prepared, quite positive all relationships you value will survive the impact of your shattering news.

My relationships with my children did not survive and I am depressed about this at some point nearly every day. I did things the wrong way particularly in the way I ended my marriage. But according to them I had been doing things the wrong way as a mother for a very long time? Had I? Perhaps.

If this is all they remember of me, the "harsh and unfair disciplining", learn from my mistakes. Just in case you initiate the ending of your marriage or relationship, be warned there is a real risk your children may forget all the good, loving and positive times. If you are a mother you are probably the main carer in the home. If you leave they may choose to forget this and remember you only as someone who limited their freedom or who set out daily chores or as someone who imposed strict guidelines for their safety, well-being and behaviour. Accusing you of being just a boring disciplinarian, they may not choose to remember how much you loved or cared for them, even when they were naughty. This could affect your mental health for some time.

Maybe we all need to be taught parenting skills before children come along. Not how to change a nappy or bath a baby but how not to be so strict with unimportant things which will just take their course. Perhaps we need to be taught more relaxed parenting and straightforward common sense in seeing our children as individuals with different needs and values. I thought I was already doing this, taking each one separately to the shop to spend birthday money, making allowances for untidy bedrooms so they could complete projects in their bedroom, ignoring untidy bedrooms for weeks and weeks, letting them off washing, cleaning their teeth on a Friday night but on no other night and going to bed on a mattress on the floor in their clothes ("camping night tonight, Mum"). Any spare money I had was spent on them. If the moon had been available to me, they could have had that too.

Barring their actual physical safety, unsociable behaviour and wanton criminal acts, perhaps I should have let them do as they liked from the moment they were born. When I think of all the intense energy used up, the emotional stresses, the anxiety levels when they were unwell, and for what? For nothing. All giving from one side and all taking on the other throws out the balance. It's wrong and brings parents to their knees, mentally and physically, particularly afterwards when all that is left are memories and isolation.

MY STORY

My former husband was witty, articulate, has a string of letters after his name (although most are bought through memberships) and enjoyed sporting success as a South of England schoolboy athletics champion, a county rugby player and a potential professional footballer when younger. He eventually achieved a professional qualification after years of part-time study. He later acquired computer skills, had brief success as a witty after-dinner speaker, was a life-and-soul-of-the-party type and generally was a larger-than-life character who relished being given the name 'Rottweiler' when he gained a reputation for "sorting out" difficult problems with contractors.

On the darker side, he has an incomplete degree, has been sacked, been made redundant, spent all the children's savings – we had none – was a drunkard, a glutton, was bombastic, arrogantly self-important, having a driving need to dominate people both at home and at work.

Emotional abusers and gifted manipulators can be cowards, too. He scarcely visited his father after he was brain-damaged following a minor operation for a hernia. He visited his mother once in hospital when she was in the final stages of Alzheimer's Disease. Not being able to bring himself to identify the body of our eldest son, I'm told he sent our second son, nearly 20, who also had to listen to the official police account of the accident, alone, while his father left the room.

Our eldest son was 22 and technically an adult when he made his Will banning me and my family from attending his funeral. My brother and father protested but my ex-husband asked his solicitors to send a fax stating he was merely carrying out our son's wishes. The executors of my son's Will (young friends) apparently had instructions to 'remove' us from the crematorium if we did turn up, despite an emotional appeal by my father and brother who tried to reason that my son was still a very young man, still maturing and still deeply angry at the break-up of his parents' marriage.

Friends say no one can take my memories away. It's easy for others to say that but difficult for me to accept. It hurts beyond description that my children have been made to suffer unnecessarily. Any good memories they might have retained of me have been desecrated and replaced by those of someone whom they now remember as "harsh and unfair". The balance sheet, in fairness and in justice, needs balancing.

For many years, I assumed I was being a good mother in a thousand ways too tedious to itemise but which included disciplining as well as making cakes, clothes, reading, singing, playing, watching football, rugby, cricket matches, admiring, scolding. Love, though, was top priority.

But after two decades of marriage to an immature, adolescent drunkard who wasted family money on hobbies or puerile business schemes, I was seriously unhappy. The care of our four children fell primarily to me during whose upbringing, over 20 years, I worked either part or full-time. I was beyond being worn out, being over-tired, over-stressed and over-worked through having to fight many wars on many fronts.

Some people seem to mature faster than their partners while the other partner seems to have stood still. Perhaps this happened to me. Some people, though, never to seem to want to change or to mature. The person to whom I was married, many years later, seemed not to be the person I remembered or imagined I had married.

It might be true the younger me disappeared a long time ago, and was replaced by a person of maturing, differing values or opinions not in step with those of my husband. In manners, aspirations and behaviour we seemed, mostly, to be poles apart.

I'd had too much of working on autopilot as a mother: shopping in my lunch-hour, loading it into my bicycle basket, wedging it in the office fridge, cycling home with it, preparing meals with it, preparing packed lunches with it, remembering family birthdays, writing thank-you letters, visiting teachers, reminding, cherishing, nagging, fussing, fretting, admiring, supporting, sustaining, cheering, jollying-along, stripping beds, loading the washing machine, forever caring, nurturing an assortment of children with strong, varied personalities, one of whom always seeming to be "going through a stage" which brought its own joys as well as problems.

I'd had enough working as a secretary in a frantically busy further education college experiencing severe funding cuts: less staff but more students. More courses taught by over-stretched tutors with little support, inadequate resourcing of classrooms, offices, computers all seemed to lead back to the secretaries manning a crowded office, dealing with dozens of telephone calls a week, working on insufficient computers – trying to satisfy too many people for too much of the time. Typing, answering telephones, dealing with personal callers, minute-taking, coming in to a over-loaded in-tray every morning was too much.

I'd had enough of studying in the evenings, during this time, to try and get a degree to lift myself out of the £5 an hour earnings of a secretary. Studying into the early hours, attending classes mainly in the evening, cycling home late at night for two years, preparing, researching material for assignments to be handed in by a deadline had all taken its toll.

I'd had enough of being the wife of someone who was ill-mannered, sullen, drunken, ill-humoured except when he was exhibiting adolescent facetiousness.

I'd had enough of living with someone who had been sacked in his working life for an "attitude problem" and now had been made redundant, for possibly the same reason, within two years. We had taken four children out of a settled school and social environment and now had nothing again. We were stranded in a strange place with little support.

I'd had enough of being his minder, his conscience:

Have you phoned my step-father to thank him for the mortgage cheque yet? I don't think it is my job, or anyone's job, but I think it would be nice to telephone him as soon as it arrives. He asked me last week if it had and I said, "Oh, didn't –. ring you?" It makes me look a completely ungrateful fool, especially as you asked him to leave it blank so you can decide who you want to pay every month.

Excusing, praising, encouraging, reassuring, cheering up, for his own self-esteem:

You've got a lot to give, OK, so you've been pushed off the track; look upon it as an opportunity others don't experience. You have a chance to think hard about what you really want to do.

Co-ercing, inciting for the benefit of the family:

I just think we should talk about moving to a smaller house, make some enquiries about renting a house. Does it really matter what other people think? Isn't it more important to be able to pay our own bills? Please don't say I'm not supporting you. I supported you financially and emotionally for the four years you've been unemployed. Living in a large house is a luxury. The world has changed, we can't afford the mortgage, you've got to look reality in the face. Looking in The Times for a job hasn't worked, you've had more than a thousand rejections. Please, please just consider me and the children for once. I don't care if you get a job in the chocolate factory or the chicken factory. You need to get a job of some sort.

Well I earn £5 an hour, why shouldn't you? Please put out the rubbish, please pick up the dog mess in the garden, please, please get any job and be nice to me. I don't care about possessions or status.

Don't disturb Daddy, he's working on the computer.

Can't you greet me, son, when you come into the house to dump your clothes by the washing machine?

So I walked out. I walked out after nearly 25 years of marriage, during which I had about one year of a happy marriage but many, many years of working to try and improve it.

He used the present divorce petitioning procedures to put down examples to illustrate my so-called unreasonable behaviour. My solicitor told me leaving the cap off the toothpaste could be cited as a reason for divorce.

Here are a few extracts from my former husband's Petition for divorce against me:

• The Respondent has indulged in an improper and inappropriate association with another man.

• The Respondent has used vile and profane language to the Petitioner in front of the children [I used the F-word for the first and only time to my 20 year old son on the night I left his father.]

• The Respondent has behaved in a violent and threatening manner to the Petitioner [cross, shouting, furious, lots of outbursts – yes – but, violent and threatening? I am 5'2", weigh 10 stone; my ex-husband is 5'9"weighs 18 stone plus; my two older sons, 18 and 20 then, nearly 6', weighed 12-14 stone. I seldom threatened my younger children but did slap my daughter across the face before her 12th birthday, and smacked them both occasionally].

• ...including making threatening gestures with a milk bottle. [I remember asking my second son, then 18 who had called in with his dirty washing, if he would put out the milk bottles I'd washed. Sometimes he would rub two together, knowing this annoyed me, to make them squeak. I remember once grabbing them, saying, "If you do that again, I'll break them over your bloody head". Perhaps that was it.]

And so the Particulars went on, citing his grievances as well as those of the children, so I felt the children, too, were divorcing me.

My own Petition, citing drunken behaviour, financial irresponsibility, emotional and physical abuse was, unfortunately, one day too late, not having taken my birth certificate with me when I left home. Cross-petitioning, however, is seldom an option. The outcome – a divorce – is the same, whatever the words and whoever does the petitioning. Few solicitors will take on a cross-petition unless you are very rich or very angry.

To me it mattered little who divorced whom. I didn't need a prize. The relief felt in just being away from him was enough: divorce was the icing on the cake.

THINK TWICE AND SEEK HELP

Think long and hard about all your options if you are absolutely serious about leaving. Take time to sit down and reflect, make lists of what makes you unhappy even if you destroy them afterwards. If you keep notes, keep them secure, preferably outside the home.

When your marriage is going wrong your mind becomes muddled with deep sadness and it is almost impossible to think logically or rationally. Find someone, preferably a professional, who will help you sort out your unhappiness and separate it into mental compartments. You may find just knowing *why* helps to isolate real problems in your mind to enable you to reflect with professional guidance on short or long-term solutions.

You might discover, by sifting through the black strands of unhappiness and finding reasons for it, a space in your mind will be cleared to carry on with an unhappy marriage for many more years.

One reason for carrying on a marriage for some people is the thought of public failure if the marriage or relationship is to be dismantled. In his book, Couples Parting, Tony Gough believes that:

"Many people are haunted by the fear of failure. There is usually a long history of this fear carried within most of us and, from time to time, the thought of adding to the catalogue of our failures is daunting. We begin to see our marriage falling about our ears and, as if that were not enough to cope with, we add to our misery the fear of failing other people. We start

to ask, 'What will we tell the children...my mother and father...my sister who always envied my marriage...the neighbours...the vicar...my colleagues at work?

The 'what-will-so-and-so think? factor keeps a lot of marriages functioning long after their 'sell-by date'. The advantages, of course, are not hard to find. It means that we can fend off those awkward questions from relatives and friends a little longer. We can also indulge in our wishful thinking that it will turn out all right in the end."

People can and do sustain imperfect relationships for years for many reasons. Sometimes it's too much effort to do anything about it. Sometimes they may feel too settled, too tired or dispirited, too old, too poor or just resigned to leaving it alone as it's too much trouble to change things and will create too much unhappiness for too many people.

Perhaps most people carry on for very practical reasons, for the sake of the children. Happily, some relationships can even improve given time, maturity, changes in attitude, financial circumstances, personal outlook or relationship counselling from professionals like Relate. You are lucky if this happens.

JOANNE'S STORY

I left my family home four and a half years ago and, like yours, my children want nothing to do with me. A day does not go by when I don't think about them and regret I did not take them with me. Like you, I thought they would be happier in their own home surrounded by their family and friends.

When I first left I thought I must have been the only mother in the world to have left her children and I felt truly evil. It took me a long, long time to come to terms with the situation and the pain has eased a little.

I think your book will help a lot of parents who are thinking of leaving. However, I must say, when it happened for me, and I decided to leave, I did not turn to the book-shelf. I only did this after the event. My leaving, my actual walking out of the door for the last time, was timed to the minute but the rest of the plan fell apart.

I have very, very good friends who helped me and are still helping me. But you are right – I burdened them and it was very difficult for them when my ex-husband called round to see them and wanted answers. They are loyal to me, they are like my sisters rather than friends, we are very close and they are my life-line to my children. Although they don't have a lot of information, as my ex does not allow the children to speak to them, they support me and would do anything for me, and me them.

The only pre-leaving advice I sought (professionally) was a free half-hour session with a local solicitor. When I told him my plan to leave, he looked at me in disbelief. The one thing I remember him saying to me was

"What will you feel at Christmas when you wake up in the morning and your children aren't there?"

It was not what I wanted to hear. I had my plan and I did not want anyone to distract me from it. I certainly would not have hunted for a book that could have changed my mind. My friends threw all sorts of questions and challenges at me, and I answered each one with confidence till, in the end, they were as convinced as I was that I was making the right decision and doing it the right way. I hurt them as much as I hurt my children, and not a day goes by when they wish they had stopped me leaving, as our lives have changed so dramatically.

I met my former husband, W., at a local disco in 1972 when I was almost 14. He was three years older than me. We had a very on-off relationship as teenagers do but in 1980 we married, bought a house and settled quite happily. In 1984 my first son, G, was born. He was a wonderful baby, and I was basically very happy although very lonely. I had worked full-time up to having him so I had made no friends in the village. W. was a shift worker and when he came in from work he either went straight to bed or straight to the pub. He worked hard, he didn't come home steaming drunk – I was lonely and wanted his company. I wanted us to go out as a family.

That year my mother became seriously ill. She ran a pub with my step-father who was twenty years her senior. He was also gravely ill with angina. The pub was closed and my mum came to live with us, my step-father went with his children. I had not got the room or the capability to look after a baby, a sick mum and my step-father as well. The events over the next year in 1985 took a great effect on our marriage. W. treated my mother as an intruder (although she was too sick to notice) and he did not lift a finger to help me. In the May she died and, the day after, my stepfather died.

A week previously my sister told me she was leaving her husband (no children) and could she come and stay with me for a while. Four weeks later I found I was pregnant again. I was at breaking point. I was traumatised and drained with the caring and coping with the death of my mum, trying to be strong and supportive to my sister, taking care of a 14 month child and then finding I was pregnant again. It was almost too much to bear.

I went to the Marriage Guidance Council alone, with G. in the pushchair, and I broke down. They were very supportive and said they could see us straightaway but W. would not go. In 1986 L. was born, a dark-haired and beautiful child. I was happier now. I had my children, I had lots of friends, ran the home and became independent. In 1987 M. was born, my loving child. He would cuddle up to me and say, "I will marry you when I grow up, Mum."

Where did it all go wrong? I don't know. W. is a 'man's man: goes out to work, earns the daily bread, expects his dinner on the table, gets ready, goes to the pub. I looked after the children, cared for the home and was thankful for my lot. Over the next 7 years my life changed. I became stronger, wanted more and enjoyed going out with my friends. W. didn't mind because I didn't interfere with what he wanted to do. We led separate lives up to a point. I was always faithful and I know W. was.

Then at Christmas in 1992 I met B. at a party. It was a girls' night out at a country hotel. B. was working in the area and staying the night there. We sat in the bar cooling off after the disco and my friend started chatting to him. She persuaded him to come into the disco with us. That's how it all began.

We started talking and talking. He gave me his phone number and we said goodbye. When I got on the minibus, I threw it away. I had enjoyed his company too much and could have been tempted. I had told him I worked evenings at a local restaurant and the Wednesday before Christmas Day he rang me there to wish me a happy Christmas. He asked me if he could see me again if he was working in the area. I hesitated then said, "Yes." I heard nothing for two months then, out of the blue, he rang me. We met and our affair began. He wanted to talk to me, listen to me, BE with me. By May I was totally obsessed and in love, and he with me. We saw each other regularly, considering the travelling distance between us. I spoke for hours each day to him.

I can put my hand on my heart and say I was not a full-time mother at this time and I think my children picked up on this long before W. did. I was a cheat and a liar but I still loved my children.

We talked constantly about living together. B. was married with two children (8 and 13) and mine were 6, 7 and 9. W. was getting suspicious and I was scared. He would have killed me if he had found out. He could be very violent. I had had a few beatings and furniture smashed in our 14 years together.

B. and I split up but, within the week, we were back together again. I couldn't bear to be without him and him me. We decided to live together. We would have Christmas with our families and planned to leave on a certain day in the new year. The day before I took my children to school and packed my clothes and my treasures of my children in the suitcase. I picked them up from school and, later in the evening when I had dropped W. at the pub, we went and got fish and chips and enjoyed them together. I kept them up late that night as I wanted to spend every extra second with them. We played cards and I said to them, "Listen, no matter what anybody says to you, always remember I love you very, very much." It went over their heads except for L.

Rightly or wrongly, I had decided to leave my children with their father in their own home, in the village they had known all their lives, with their grandma, granddad, aunt, uncle and friends close by. I thought they would hate me more to take them away to an unknown destination with a man they had never met.

I hugged and kissed them forever that night. When W. came in I was asleep. The next morning he got up early to go to work and I said goodbye. He told me later that, that morning he felt something was wrong and nearly came home early. I took the children to school. M. hugged and laughed, going in and waved forever through the window. My heart was breaking inside. I took L. and G. to the junior school. L. went to his class and G. had a family assembly until 9.30. He was so proud doing his little bit in front of me, then they filed into class. As I was leaving, L. rushed out of class and clung to me. "Mum", he said, "I was scared with what you said last night." I reassured him and he went back, hesitatingly.

He waved to me through the window, all along the road until I was out of sight. That picture and those memories will haunt me until the day I die.

I went home, heart-broken, scared, excited, focused. I rang B. and he was on his way. He had left his wife the previous evening and I could tell he felt the same as me. But we were in love and still thought this was the best way.

I rang a family friend to ask him to ask my mother-in-law to pick the children up from school and told him I was leaving W. He told me to take care of myself and he would collect the children. I don't think he realised I was going for good at the time. I left a letter for my mother-in-law and one for W. I could not find the words to write one for the children but hoped to see them shortly and explain to them in person. A taxi came a few moments later, dropping me off half a mile away where B. was waiting for me and we left together.

It was four weeks before I saw the children again. It was Mother's Day. They greeted me shyly, apprehensively, hugged and kissed me and gave me cards and flowers. I put the Mother's Day cards up each year as I did not receive any more. I asked W. if I could take the children out, talk to them, explain to them but he wouldn't let me take them out of his sight. The children clung to his side. They were scared of losing him, too.

Over the next few months it was a nightmare. I travelled up constantly to see the children and slowly, they were turning against me. W. wanted me back, he was still in love with me -he still is. I didn't love him – I felt sorry for him – I knew if I went back I would eventually leave again and cause the children pain yet again. The pain was almost killing me.

I then made the biggest mistake of all. After a very fretful, tearful day with W. and the boys I said I would go back. And I really meant it. I was swallowed up with hurt, grief and pain and I could not take any more. B. was waiting for me to pick me up and drive back home. I got in the car and told him I was staying. We hugged, cried and held each other for ages. He asked me to come back for a few days and I agreed.

B. told his children I was going back. We had already met and got on quite well, considering. The next few days were a blur. I was torn apart and felt almost suicidal. I had told W. I would be back by Friday but by Wednesday I knew I would be making a big mistake by going back. Things would never be the same again. I rang him and told him I would not be coming home.

I had built up my children's hopes and hurt them so badly yet again.

Later, W. told me and the social worker that, on the Friday I was supposed to have gone back, W. had taken the boys fishing. L. looked up at him an said, "We will have to get home soon, dad, and tidy up because mum's coming home." J said, "No, son, she's not coming home." L. then just sobbed quietly for a very long time. I know this is W's interpretation but that picture will go with me to my grave.

I was not allowed to see my children, speak to them (an answering machine was installed) and all communication was stopped. Over the next three and a half years I have struggled through the courts for access. The courts have no powers and my children had suffered enough. I did not want them being interviewed by complete strangers. So, in the end, and £10,000 lighter, I gave up.

For B., things worked out as he predicted. His wife was very reasonable. She wanted him to have as much to do with the children as possible. We live 5 miles away from them, compared to the 200 miles to mine and they visit us weekly. They have their own bedrooms and come on holiday with us. They were upset at the beginning but have adjusted well. That could have happened with mine but it didn't.

Sometimes when I'm low or depressed I get angry with B. He still has his children, his job, his friends. Nothing much changed for him. I get resentful and bitter. I am a changed person. I am not the woman B. first met. B. loves me, I know he does, but I sometimes wonder if he wishes he could turn the clock back, for my sake. Most of the time we are so very, very happy but when the dark times come it is usually because of my situation. We have made our beds and now we must lie in them. I love B. deeply and he is very strong and supportive. He would give or do anything for me but he can't give me the one thing I need – my children.

There are the beginnings of a turning point but I don't hold my breath any more. I have had too many let-downs. My only hope is one day one of them will call me or write to me – be it 5, 10 or 20 years' time. I can only hope and pray. I hope your book will help women who want to leave because they are being abused and need help financially or they need a plan to escape. For me, I don't know. I wrote my own book – the book of life and, unfortunately, that cannot be re-written.

EMOTIONALLY ABUSED CHILDREN DURING SEPARATION AND DIVORCE

"All families are made up of individuals who live together in relatively stable intimate groups with the ostensible purpose of supporting and caring for each other. Family members develop their own rules and boundaries, spoken and unspoken, about the ways that they will behave with each other, support and care for each other. Each family's rules and boundaries change over time to reflect modifications in membership, the evolving needs of its members and the realities of the outer world.

Most changes in the family system are gradual but some events force cataclysmic upheaval. Divorce is usually such an event....As a member of the family system, a child is attached legally, emotionally and psychologically to each of his parents. As a member of a divorce impasse system, a child is often asked to ally himself with one parent or the other, a request which clearly places the child in a loyalty bind."

Peggie Ward, J. Campbell Harvey, Family Wars.

In the United Kingdom, there are books, pamphlets, leaflets advertising and supporting what could be described as a lucrative sector of commerce: the legal and professional counselling and conciliation sectors which underpin separation, splitting up, and finally divorce. The process of un-doing a marriage brings you into many different fields of professionals, offering many services after divorce, and supporting families through the trauma.

Had I been in the right frame of mind to search I might have found a few books, web sites and counsellors to help make up my mind on the right way to end a marriage, the right words to say to my husband or how to do it to lessen the savage impact on our children.

There would have been few books however offering graphic warnings on the dangers of leaving my husband suddenly and ill-prepared and who would then assist my children into becoming irreversibly brain-washed into hating me for leaving him.

Divorce is an alarming and shocking word. It is the big D. It is a word which some people even sub-consciously or consciously aware of their deep unhappiness and who are seriously thinking of ending their own relationship, cannot bring themselves to use. Associated with the world of TV soaps, media personalities, royalty, movie stars, it is consigned to a place in our minds labelled "things that happen to other people but not to me".

Once it does happen to you, it brings terror, panic and a feeling of intense bleakness. Imagine therefore its impact on your children whose completely safe world with two parents has come apart.

To hear it used for the very first time in your own situation perhaps by a counsellor or solicitor, and then to use it yourself – almost then as part of everyday language – is a shock you hoped would never come your way even if you have initiated it. Divorce can be such a major blow, such a catastrophically negative force like a road collision, some people suffer real trauma and need help for a very long time afterwards.

Children need help to cope with such a major catastrophe in their safe world but few get it even though it is there if one knows where to search on their behalf. Children of all ages take refuge in silence and because some will not or cannot articulate their grief, people assume that they are just "accepting" the situation. Much help and sympathy seems to aimed at the parent who has not initiated the divorce and who appears at first to be the one who carries the major part of its burden of suffering.

Some children are terrified their parents' divorce might somehow be their fault. Traumatised by a burgeoning horror occurring in their own safe family world they become either withdrawn or angry, lashing at the one parent who seems to have instigated the mess thereby becoming easily receptive to the beginning of an indoctrination programme. Everyone wants to blame someone. But to involve blameless children who have very little or nothing to do with why their parents' relationship or marriage is ending is morally indefensible.

In one of many United States-based web sites on the Internet supporting divorced parents and families, www.SmartDivorce.com ("Your divorce learning center for Practical Solutions to Divorce") promote the Total Parenting Handbook by Terry Hillman, Pam Weintraul. In their introduction the authors believe that

> *"Divorce is a time when you are necessarily focused on your own feelings. It is often difficult to think about anything but what is happening to you. Whether you have been surprised to find out that your marriage is coming to an end or you have been the one contemplating the separation for months, severing this primary relationship is all encompassing.*

> *But if you have children, you have a dual responsibility – to yourself, yes, but most important, to your kids. Keep in mind that you are an adult with the perspective of an adult. Children cannot put things into perspective. Your children know only the security and love they have had with the parents who have nurtured and guided them throughout their short lives. When these are threatened, children become fearful and anxious. The thought of losing one or even both parents is frightening. The other life changes your children may come to experience from moving residences to adjusting to a stepfamily would disorient even the strongest, most experienced adult.*

> *Your primary function now is to help your children cope with all of these changes even as you deal with the pain and turmoil inside you. You must be a rock, a comforter, a listener, a protector. You must rise above your own feelings and think about your children first, just as you've been doing all along, because that is what parenting is all about."*

Emotional abuse of children is often an unnamed destructive side issue but it is an abuse as potentially injurious as sexual or physical abuse and should be highlighted by all involved in divorce litigation where children are affected. Dr. Richard Gardner (see Parental Alienation Syndrome later) believes that PAS or emotional abuse is indeed a form of child abuse and should be acknowledged as such:

> *"It is important for examiners to appreciate that a parent who inculcates PAS in a child is indeed perpetrating a form of emotional abuse in that*

such programming may not only produce lifelong alienation from a loving parent, but lifelong psychiatric disturbance in the child. A parent who systematically programs a child into a state of on-going denigration and rejection of a loving and devoted parent is exhibiting complete disregard of the alienated parent's role in the child's upbringing. Such an alienating parent is bringing about a disruption of a psychological bond that could, in the vast majority of cases, prove of great value to the child – the separated and divorced status of the parents notwithstanding.

Accordingly, courts do well to consider the PAS programming parent to be exhibiting a serious parental deficit when weighing the pros and cons of custodial transfer. I am not suggesting that a PAS-inducing parent should automatically be deprived of primary custody, only that such induction should be considered a serious deficit in parenting capacity – a form of emotional abuse – and that it be given serious consideration when weighing the custody decision. In this book, I provide specific guidelines regarding the situations when such transfer is not only desirable, but even crucial, if the children are to be protected from lifelong alienation from the targeted parent."

Peggie Ward believes that

"It is psychologically harmful to children to be deprived of a healthy relationship with one parent. There is substantial research that indicates children need contact with adults of both sexes for balanced development."

She believes the motivation for alienation usually stems from the alienating parent having

"strong underlying feelings and emotions left over from earlier unresolved emotional issues which have been resuscitated and compounded by the pain of the divorce. The individual, in attempting to ward off these powerful and intensely uncomfortable feelings, develops behavioural strategies that involve the children.

One solution to the pain and anger is to sue for custody of the child and to endeavour to punish the other parent by seeking his or her exclusion. The internal world of an alienating parent can have complex origins."

She concludes that:

"The persistent quality of the conflict combined with its enduring nature, seriously endangers the mental health of the parents and the psychological development of the children. Under the guise of fighting for the child, the parents may succeed in inflicting severe emotional suffering on the very person whose protection and well-being is the presumed rationale for the battle.

Alienation occurs when the parties to divorce or custody litigation use their children to meet their own emotional needs as vehicles to express or carry their intense emotions or as pawns to manipulate as a way of inflicting retribution on the other side. The focus in determining whether or not there is alienation in an angry divorce must be not on the degree of rage more or less expressed, but on behavioural willingness to involve children."

In the current field of European or UK legislation and public awareness we appear to be light years away from a situation where legislators, judges, solicitors, barristers or divorce court welfare officers in the United Kingdom or other professionals elsewhere in Europe will do anything but admit, in very few instances, that Parental Alienation Syndrome exists in the United States but no where else, let alone is acknowledged as an important condition having potentially devastating consequences for our children's future mental health and emotional well-being. They may just acknowledge, without giving it a syndromic name, that a certain set of circumstances may arise in high-conflict divorces whereby children are emotionally damaged but many relationships with children outside marriage break up and for these children the same set of circumstances will also occur. Emotional damage caused to children in high-conflict family splits, whether their parents are married or not, is certain.

It is a situation that should be rectified. It should be widely debated in public as well as addressed in the legal and judicial system. It should be given formal acknowledgement on our Statute Book so it exists. It should be as illegal to abuse children emotionally as it is illegal to abuse them physically.

Parental Alienation Syndrome should be something from which courts and responsible parents should protect children, legally and emotionally, and for which the alienated parent should be able to claim legal redress through the courts on behalf of the children involved. The right to hold both parents in equal esteem until the child reaches the age of judgmental maturity should become part of the United Nations Charter of Children's Rights.

Dr. Gardner further believes that:

"There are some who claim that the PAS is not really a syndrome. This criticism, like many, is especially seen in courts of law in the context of child-custody disputes. It is an argument sometimes promulgated by those who claim that PAS does not even exist. The PAS is a very specific disorder. A syndrome, by medical definition, is a cluster of symptoms, occurring together, that characterise a specific disease. The symptoms, although seemingly disparate, warrant being grouped together because of a common etiology or basic underlying cause.

Furthermore, there is a consistency with regard to this cluster in that most (if not all) of the symptoms appear together. Accordingly, there is a kind of purity that syndrome has that may not be seen in other diseases. For example, a person suffering with pneumococcal pneumonia may have chest pain, cough, purulent sputum, and fever. However, the individual may still have the disease without all these symptoms manifesting themselves. The syndrome is more often "pure" because most (if not all) of the symptoms in the cluster predictably manifest themselves."

Dr. Gardner goes on:

"Similarly, the PAS is characterised by a cluster of symptoms that usually appear together in the child, especially in the moderate and severe types. These include:

1 A campaign of denigration.

2 Weak, absurd, or frivolous rationalisations for the deprecation.

3 Lack of ambivalence.

4 The "independent-thinker" phenomenon.

5   Reflexive support of the alienating parent in the parental conflict.

6   Absence of guilt over cruelty to and/or exploitation of the alienated parent.

7   The presence of borrowed scenarios.

8   Spread of the animosity to the friends and/or extended family of the alienated parent.

Typically, children who suffer with PAS will exhibit most (if not all) of these symptoms. This is almost uniformly the case for the moderate and severe types. However, in the mild cases one might not see all eight symptoms. When mild cases progress to moderate or severe, it is highly likely that most (if not all) of the symptoms will be present. This consistency results in PAS children resembling one another. It is because of these considerations that the PAS is a relatively "pure" diagnosis that can easily be made by those who are not somehow blocked from seeing what is right in front of them. As is true of other syndromes, there is an underlying cause: programming by an alienating parent in conjunction with additional contributions by the programmed child. It is for these reasons that PAS is indeed a syndrome, and it is a syndrome by the best medical definition of the term."

After divorce or splitting up, and having experienced the temporary or permanent alienation of their own children using whatever syndrome or appendage one may care to choose, people become experts of their own situation, the legal minefield and their children's reactions. By then it's far too late to have acquired that knowledge.

Lives are ripped apart for a long time if divorce follows a familiar 20th century pattern. Some lives are ruined forever if contact with children is severed for many years. The loss of precious years of childhood, not just for the absent parent but more importantly for the child experiencing his/her loss, is significant and potentially injurious for that child's future image of his/her own role in society as a parent. Those years can never be made good even if the children came back after 5, 10 or 15 years. For the absent parent the deprivation of time apart from cherished children is like a everlasting bereavement set in stone. For the children, it means a lifetime of adjustment to serious emotional problems. In Caught in the Middle, Carla B. Garrity and Mitchell A. Baris report that:

> *"Aggression, behaviour problems and depression are frequent early responses to being caught in the middle of continuing animosity between parents. Later in life, too, the children of high-conflict divorce are very likely to suffer serious emotional problems. Ten to fifteen years after a divorce, such children report haunting memories, especially of episodes of physical violence.*
>
> *Conflict does not, however, need to be physical to be harmful to children. For children, conflict is any situation that places them between their parents or that forces them to choose between them. Being in the middle means anything from hearing one parent belittle the other's values to vicious verbal attacks; from threats of violence to actual violence."*

Distressing accounts of the appallingly painful impact on children of splitting up, harrowing stories of parents who lose contact, should begin to be a thing of the past if parents themselves could think about embracing radical new ideas on how to deal with the un-doing of a relationship when children are involved. Children should be the first people they think about, not the last, when they want to split up.

That all-important Residence Order (previously custody) often represents a hollow victory over the other partner over whom we wave the scalps of our children, contaminating their image of the other.

- Could we ever consider placing Parental Alienation Syndrome on our Statute Book and make it an offence to brain-wash our children, emotionally, against one parent?

- Could we ever consider, in the New Millennium, throwing away forever archaic ideas concerning ownership of children – after divorce?

"Ownership" of children, whether by a Residence Order in the United Kingdom or custody in the United States is still deeply ingrained in society's mind as being a fundamentally important end-product of the divorce process whereby one party, sometimes the one who has not initiated the actual divorce or split, must be seen to be the winner of children's hearts, minds and physical presence if the divorce is to be a "successful" one and the aggrieved party can be seen to retain some post-divorce dignity.

Another web site on the Internet actively promotes the importance of "ownership of children" by its very name, www.winchildcustody.com and is dedicated to:

> *"teaching you how to WIN OR DEFEND CUSTODY for your child. ...We will teach you what you need to know about child custody. We will tell you ahead of time what your attorney may not tell you. Stay one step ahead of the process to achieve success."*

www.winchildcustody.com will even sell you a 90-minute video seminar at $34.95 to:

> *"help you prevent costly mistakes you cannot afford to make with your child."*

If current changes in the divorce laws in the United Kingdom are enacted, the legal system will discard where appropriate any discussion of victimisation, anger, destruction, sabotage and revenge which the two main protagonists formerly dragged through the courts, using it as a place to voice personal wounds in a marriage which had simply come to an end. Formerly both sides used the excuse of children's best interests to fight for their rights in expensive courts while using a gloves-off approach, exposing all the faults but none of the attributes. In so doing children inevitably become brainwashed. The ending of this has got to be a good thing for our children. But it will not stop emotional abuse taking place by the aggrieved parent.

- Could we accept dual parenting as a real workable possibility in the 21st century?

Arthur Baker, Lecturer in Social Policy, Barnsley College, and Peter Townsend, Senior Lecturer in Law, University of Teesside believe that

> *"Shared residence is the idea that, following divorce or separation, mothers and fathers should retain a strong positive parenting role in their*

children's lives, with the children actually spending substantial amounts of time living with each parent....Interest in shared residence has increased for a number of reasons. There has been a growing awareness of the effect of divorce on children."

In outlining the role of the judicial system in acknowledging this, they state:

"The Children Act 1989 gave some further hope to advocates of shared residence. Under section 11(4) it became possible for courts to make joint residence orders. The Act states:

'Where a Residence Order is made in favour of two or more persons who do not themselves live together, the order may specify the periods during which the child is to live in the different households concerned'.

This point is reinforced in regulations and guidance, which state that: 'a shared Residence Order could ... be made where the child is to spend, for example, weekdays with one parent and weekends with the other or term time with one parent and school holidays with the other, or where the child is to spend large amounts of time with each parent.'

The guidance goes on to say that:

'a shared care order has the advantage of being more realistic in those cases where the child spends considerable amounts of time with both parents, brings with it certain other benefits, and removes any impression that one parent is good and responsible whereas the other parent is not.'

However, Messrs. Baker and Townsend comment on the role of divorce court welfare officers in promoting this guidance:

"In the UK, social work assistance to the family courts is provided by the Court Welfare Service, itself an arm of the Probation Service. British Court Welfare Officers have not been proactive in arguing the case for shared parenting. A National Association of Probation Officers' policy document on the role of the Court Welfare Officer does not address the issue of shared residence adequately, in spite of its many references to gender equality; neither is the issue addressed in the recent Home Office strategy document

on the future of the Court Welfare Service or in the recently published national standards for the Court Welfare Service."

Consider the enriching impact dual-parenting might have on the lives of both children and parents as opposed to ripping children apart when they are made to choose one parent. (This presupposes, always, the choice of school, religion, home locations have been settled and established well beforehand by both parents through lengthy discussion, negotiation and, eventually, agreement. In some unique situations, however, one parent might have to retain the final word.)

A quick trawl of the Internet, using the search words 'Divorce' and 'Counselling', reveals the United States as being at the frontier of accepting marriage break-up as largely inescapable in such a hugely diversified society but, equally, that damage limitation is vital for children and their future well-balanced lives.

The changing pattern of late 20th century family life critically demonstrates that we must all accept marriage or partnership breakdown in the 21st century as statistically inevitable, and that divorce and splitting up a family should almost be viewed as a continuous process of normal life. 'Normal' life in the future for our children will probably mean marriage, separation, divorce and re-marriage or a second partnership for the nuclear family as well as many other types and variations of partnerships.

It is, whether we like it or not, an undeniable part of our own evolving multi-cultural, divergent society in the United Kingdom as well as in the rest of the world.

The United States leads the world in having set up a burgeoning industry of post-divorce counselling and education programmes for families involved in separation and divorce. The Children of Separation and Divorce Center, Incorporated have published Guidelines for Child-focused Decision Making, a Manual for Judges, Attorneys, Mediators, Mental Health Professionals and Parents Concerning Children of Divorce.

The Guidelines were written:

"with the goals of helping judges, attorneys, mediators and mental health

professionals address the critical factors relating to decision-making about children's healthy functioning from infancy through adolescence".

They believe:

"regardless of the kind of therapy children are involved in, all appropriate significant others in the family are involved at specified times to support the child and changes being made to help the family."
(http://cosd.bayside.net/about.htm)

No morally principled parent involved in splitting up a relationship or marriage sets out to wreak such havoc in the lives of their children that those children need therapy from outside sources. However, in the event that children do need help most responsible parents would want to follow these guidelines in involving everyone in the family, grandparents, aunts and uncles, cousins, as well as both parents and siblings, in supporting their children through emotional changes which threaten the stability of family life and their children's place in that family life.

It is sound advice which all conscientious, wise and dedicated parents would choose to follow for their children's sakes, regardless of any antagonistic feelings towards their partner and completely disregarding which one has initiated the break-up of the marriage or partnership.

A child's family is for life, not just while his parents remain together. A child's relationships within his family must not be allowed to disintegrate because of the malice of one paranoid parent unable to come to terms with a broken relationship or a failed marriage.

MARGARET'S STORY

I congratulate you on the courage you have shown in writing your book. I just couldn't stop reading it and found I could relate to a lot of what was said. I also cried buckets and buckets and would not settle until I had written my own story. I found this very therapeutic, realising I have needed to do this for a long time.

I wish you every success with your book. I know many will be able to relate to it as issues relating to children should not be swept under the carpet. I cannot believe how many people think I have done something terrible because my children have been taken away from me. I begin to wonder myself sometimes but I do know, deep down, I have always done my best for my children.

As an accountant, I moved to Yorkshire from Scotland in 1982 to obtain work, met my husband, a farmer, and we married in 1985. Looking back, I feel I was conned. Perhaps I needed to be loved, he was a bit like my father and, above all, a charmer. Things went well to begin with, we lived in my flat sharing household responsibilities and I continued to work full-time. In 1986 we moved to the farmhouse, formerly his parents' home, and my troubles began. He seemed to revert back to being a little boy with demands. It was as if he had always been allowed to be like this in that house. I was also badly criticised by his parents and felt my home was not my own. I had to compromise by not throwing out furniture, carpets, etc. which I detested. There was uproar when I tried to dig up roses his parents had received as a silver wedding present – I could not understand why they didn't take them when they moved.

I continued to work part-time but suffered gynaecological problems, taking a few months out. I set up business on my own from home but continued to suffer ill-health. In 1988 my daughter was born. I was continually sick for the first four months, ending up in hospital. My mother-in-law told me I had the wrong attitude and should get out of bed. She even rang my parents to tell them I was pretending.

I built up my practice to the stage where I had to move to the nearest town, becoming a partner in a small practice with which I merged. I didn't have the option of staying at home with the children as my husband's parents were in control of his finances and it was a constant battle to get them to allow him to draw a decent living from the business in which he is a partner. When I left, he only had a business chequebook when they were on holiday.

After a horrendous pregnancy resulting in infection, continuing illness, gynaecological and PMT problems, my son was born in 1984 and I had ten months off. During that summer my husband played cricket all weekend, most evenings and anytime he was asked. I remember his coming home, putting the chip pan on (I would be instantly sick), eating his meal and then going out again without coming upstairs to see or speak to me. I could not drive during the pregnancy and we lived three miles from anywhere at the end of the country lane. He continued to play cricket after the baby was born.

After I went back to work I remember coming home from work to a kitchen like a bomb site, the kids going mad and him sitting in front of the TV with a packet of biscuits most evenings. The emotional abuse I received from him and his parents got worse. I lost confidence. In November 1995 I persuaded him to go to Relate, realising our marriage was in serious difficulties. I was very concerned about its effects on my children. It appeared to go well in the sessions but as soon as we were alone he would have a go at me about things he perceived were my fault. In 1996 I remember him trying to smother me a few times but he said I was dreaming. I know it was real.

In March, the weekend before the Dunblane tragedy, he raped me. I thought I was going to die, I could not breathe and, afterwards, was covered in bruises. I was numb for weeks afterwards both because of this as well as Dunblane as my family home is seven miles from there.

On 5 May 1996 I went to my doctor and cried and cried and cried. He told me I should not go back home as he felt I was in grave danger and that I should get the children out too. I phoned the children's nanny, told her to pack a few bags and we all stayed with her that night. I saw a solicitor and went to stay with my parents in Scotland for a few days.

With hindsight, I should have stayed there but I felt it was important that the children see their father and that I continue my commitment to my business. I moved with the children in August 1997 and the children had regular contact with their father and waited for the divorce. I had huge financial problems trying to pay for proper childcare, the mortgage and carry on the business. My husband continued to terrify me, abusing me in front of the children, clients, my staff and his father even physically attacked me one day over the car I had taken when I left. I had a panic alarm installed by the police during the run-up to the divorce and help from Victim Support. I was an outcast in the community where I had always been an outsider.

On Easter Day 1997, the whole congregation in the village church (I continued to go as I was a Sunday School teacher) turned their back on me when both my ex-husband and his parents prevented my children from coming over to talk to me. He only ever went to church at Christmas and Easter. Just after this he reported me to Social Services for shouting too much at the children. It cost me £2,000 in legal fees to get them off my back and I did get an apology.

I insisted we try mediation to try to resolve our finances but this ended in disaster when he started to 'touch me up' under the table and demanded I pay him the amount he had paid for the deposit on the house I was living in. In October 1997 we were divorced, the divorce judge told me I would have to earn more money. This meant I would have to give up my business. My ex-husband, got legal aid, the CSA assessment was determined at £6, I protested but the CSA have no remit to investigate and I had to accept the figure.

I had spent £13,000 on legal fees, had to realise some of the capital I had invested in my own business to survive and was eventually head-hunted by a big practice in Edinburgh. I made plans to move there last summer, my ex-husband then made an application for a Residence Order on legal aid, a Court Welfare Officer's report was prepared in two weeks but she chose to accept my ex-husband's side of the story. She did not check up with my doctor, health visitor, vicar, police, social services or nursery school but did ring my daughter's school and misrepresented the headmistress in her report.

According to the judge, I was a very good mother and had planned the move to make everything as smooth as possible for the children. However, he felt that the nanny was more important for their continuity and because my daughter wanted to stay in Yorkshire, granted my ex-husband a Residence Order. I was utterly devastated and had to be physically removed from Court as I could not stop screaming. When I eventually got home, he had telephoned to say what had happened and that my daughter was celebrating.

I am now living near Edinburgh on my own. I see my children every third weekend for a weekend and half the school holidays. I have to travel down to Yorkshire by train to collect them and bring them back up. I feel it is important that we spend as much time as possible here and I think they are beginning to realise that it's not a bad place. They have made friends and also see something of their cousins.

On top of the travelling I have had horrendous problems sorting out the access dates with my ex-husband and am now going back to Court for Defined Access.

I have found out he leaves both children locked in the house every morning before they go to school to enable him to do his work on the farm. As a result, my daughter is bullying my son. I feel she probably resents having the responsibility of looking after her brother. I am really worried about my son. His sister is very cruel to him. He is very quiet but I can see it in his eyes – especially when we say goodbye. He is a loveable little boy and wants lots of cuddles when I see him. I feel very sad that nobody took his needs into consideration.

My number one priority at present is to make sure that contact is maintained and that my children continue to be reminded that their mother and her family loves them very dearly. However, my family has found my situation very difficult and I do spare them some problems. They are always there, I need their help and support most when I have the children and feel it is important to involve them in positive ways and not to get bogged down with grief and negative thoughts.

I don't know where my journey will end but my faith and friends have kept me strong. If there is anyone out there who has had a similar experience, I would love to hear from them. I do hope my experience can, in some way, make someone's else's journey that little bit easier.

Emotional Abuse – The Process

Peggie Ward of PACE (Advisory Council of the Professional Academy of Custody Evaluators, USA) has sub-divided alienation into four categories:

- mild
- moderate
- overt
- severe

"Examples of mild forms of alienating behaviour include:

- Little regard for the importance of visitation/contact with the other parent: "You're welcome to visit with Mom: you make the choice, I won't force you." No encouragement of visits. No concern over missed visits. No interest in the child's activities or experiences during visitation.
- Lack of value regarding communication between visits. No encouragement of communication between visits. Little awareness of the distress a child may feel if a visit or phone call is missed.
- Inability to tolerate the presence of the other parent even at events important to the child. "I won't go to any soccer games if your mother is there."
- Disregard for the importance of the relationship to the child. Displaying a willingness to apply for and accept a new job away from the other parent without regard to the child's relationship with that parent."

"Examples of moderate forms of alienating behaviour include:

- Communications of dislike of visitation: "You can visit with your Dad, but you know how I feel about it." "How can you go to see your father when you know I've been sick; Aunt B. is here..." "Visitation with your Dad is really up to you."
- Refusal to hear anything about the other parent (especially if it is good): "That's between you and your father"[regarding reports of visitation, plans for visitation]. "I don't want to hear about..."[what you did with your mother] [especially if it was fun].

- Delights in hearing negative news about the other parent.
- Refusal to speak directly with the other parent. When the target parent calls, gives the phone to the child, "It's him," in a disgusted tone of voice. Hangs up phone on the target parent. Silently hands the phone to the child when target parent is calling.
- Refusal to allow the target parent physically near. Target parent not allowed out of the car or even on the property, in the driveway, for pick-up and drop-off visitations.
- Doing and undoing statements. Negative comments about the other parent made and then denied: "There are things I could tell you about your mother but I'm not that kind of person." "Your Dad is an alcoholic, oh, I shouldn't have said that."
- Subtle accusations: "Your Dad wasn't around a lot when you were little." "Your Dad abandoned me."
- Destruction of memorabilia of the target person.

Peggie Ward also gives examples of overt alienation:

"The alienating parent is obsessed and sees the target as noxious to himself or herself, the children, and even the world. A history of the marriage is related which reflects nothing but the bad times. The target parent was never worthwhile as a spouse or a parent and is not worthwhile today. Such a parent shows little response to logic and little ability to confront reality. Many alienating parents, at this stage, entertain the overt belief that the target parent presents an actual danger of harm to the children. They present this belief as concrete knowledge that if the children spend time with the target parent they will be irreparably harmed in some manner or that they will be brainwashed by the target parent not to value/love the alienating parent.

Statements about the target parent are delusional or false:

- "Your Mom doesn't pay support" when there is evidence to show payment. "Your father doesn't love us (or "you") when there is no evidence to that effect. "Your mother drinks too much", "uses drugs", "smokes", etc. when there is no evidence to support these statements.

Inclusion of the children as victims of the target parent's bad behaviour:

- "Your Mom abandoned us." "Your Dad doesn't love us (or you) anymore."

Over-criticism of the target parent:

- "Your Mom is a drug addict/alcoholic/violent person..." "What's wrong with your Dad? He never/always does..." "Your mother endangers your health." "Your father doesn't take good care of you/doesn't feed you/take you to the doctor/understand you during visits."

The children are required to keep secrets from the target parent:

- "Don't tell your Mom where you've been/who you've seen/where you're going, etc."

Threat of withdrawal of love:

- "I won't love you if you...(see your Dad, etc.)." "I'm the only one who really loves you."

Extreme lack of courtesy to the target parent.

There is also a fourth stage of alienation, the severe stage, which is where my children started from. They had no need to go through the mild, moderate or overt stages having had no contact with me whatsoever after a week we spent together in July 1996. My ex-husband had successfully initiated them into the extreme end of the spectrum from the very beginning.

Peggie Ward states:

"By the severe stage, the alienating parent no longer needs to be active. In terms of the motivation, the alienating parent holds no value at all for the other parent (whether motivated by fears, emptiness, helplessness) and the hatred and disdain are completely overt. The alienating parent will do anything to keep the children away from the target parent.

At this stage the child is so enmeshed with the alienating parent that he or she agrees totally that the target parent is a villain and the scum of the earth. The child takes on the alienating parent's desires, emotions and hatreds and verbalises them to all as his own. The child, too, sees the history of the target parent and family as all negative and is able to neither remember nor express any positive feeling for the target parent."

MARION'S STORY

I found your story profoundly moving. It is good to see something positive has come out of all your pain and that other parents will perhaps benefit from your experience. I think you are right about the lack of advice, support and information pre-divorce. This was certainly true in my own case. If only I had known then what I know now things could have been very different. I identified with a lot of what you went through before you left, as you will see from my story.

On August Bank Holiday Monday 1997, I walked out on my husband of 16 years, leaving behind my two children, then aged 4 and 10. These are the stark facts but they are far from the whole story.

My marriage was never particularly happy. I had long since resigned myself to this and found comfort in my hobbies, my job and, of course, my children.

As the years went by, I found it increasingly difficult to cope with my husband's behaviour. He was frequently drunk and abusive, threatening me verbally with bottles and, on one occasion, with a knife. He often raised his hand as if to hit me and constantly threatened to kill himself or cause problems for me at work if I did not do what he wanted. I never knew what his mood would be like from one day to the next. I lived in constant fear and dreaded coming home from work in the evenings.

I tried many times to end the marriage but he always managed to make me change my mind through threats, emotional blackmail and by getting the children to beg and plead with me.

By the summer of 1997 he had managed to turn both children against me (he had the time to do this as he was the main carer whilst I went out to work). He would tell the children, "she's not your mother" or "she doesn't love you". He referred to me as "the bitch" to the extent that my four-year old daughter also began to refer to me as such. I was forbidden to speak to or even look at the children. I could not cook for them or take them out. He took them to sleep with him in the main bedroom leaving me to sleep in the children's room.

I was, by this time, in a state of desperation and utter misery. With my relationship with the children effectively non-existent, I felt that I had no choice but to leave and seek a legal solution from the outside.

Once I had left (which I was only able to do with police help), my overwhelming emotion was one of relief. To this day I still do not regret my action although the price has been high.

Almost two years on, I am still fighting a legal battle to secure proper contact with my children who are now 6 and 12. It is a long, hard, slow, uphill struggle but things are gradually improving and I now am able to spend a few precious hours with my children most Sundays.

The circumstances, however, remain far from ideal. My now ex-husband is as hostile as ever and both children remain firmly under his control and subject to his manipulation. They are unable to show any affection for me. They do not call me "Mummy". At times they have even kicked me and spat on me. They don't answer my letters and refuse to speak on the telephone. The other day I saw them and their father by chance in the street. They ignored my "hello" and walked straight past me as if I was a complete stranger.

Leaving my children was, and is, desperately painful but I don't regret doing what I did. I will never give up trying to re-establish a relationship with them and I hope that one day they will come to understand that I do love them.

***

JUDITH'S STORY

My circumstances aren't exactly the same as yours but I can certainly identify with some. It's quite comforting knowing you aren't the only one going through so much pain.

After nearly 24 years of marriage, I left my husband in January 1998 and moved in with another man whom I had known for a year but only very closely for 3 months. My sons, then aged 18 and 21, were aware of problems in my marriage. The youngest one had just left home for university and has proven to be loyal to both of us. However, on the other hand, my eldest son, who still lives at home, is quite "anti-me". I saw him a few times in the early stages when we met to eat out. Lately, the last month, he has made no contact with me, despite the fact I kept ringing, faxing, etc, trying to reassure him I loved him and hadn't walked out on him.

As a mum, I find it so hard to cope with the fact that I may have lost my role as a mother to him. I want him to make a move towards me. I still hurt and I need love back. To add to that pain, my parents have almost reacted the same way. I rang them, wrote to them, visited them, but all I get back is the odd letter.

The last words from my husband were, "You leave home, you lose your family." At the moment, that's what it feels like. Everyone assures me "they'll come round" but what gives my husband the right to say that?

I am very happy with the new man in my life. He's made my life so rich and content. My marriage had not always been an unhappy one but I knew in recent years it wouldn't last. No one can accept the fact I didn't leave my home and marriage for no real reason. One day I hope they will understand I did what I had to do.

I wish you a happy life and hope, in time, your children will accept what's happened and let you live your life, with them still needing you as a mum.

July 1998
Since writing the above, my circumstances have changed somewhat. My youngest son is coming over today to where I now live for the first time and hopefully will stay to meet my new partner. The eldest son is on holiday and has

said he will visit me when he returns. My main problem now is my parents. I went to see them on Sunday as they have always refused to see me in my new home. It is still very apparent they can't accept the situation and will only see me if I visit them – alone. I am finding "parental rejection of this type very difficult to understand.

December 1998

Life is changing somewhat. My parents have met my partner and we have visited them on a couple of occasions. One of the main reasons my parents agreed to meet my partner was that he wrote them a very moving letter, from the heart, introducing himself and telling them what I had actually gone through emotionally since leaving home. We also met my youngest son for dinner without problems. My eldest son still has a few problems. He won't visit me at home or meet my partner. I meet him for meals out but it comes mostly from my instigation. He's fine talking to me. It's my birthday today and I did get a card and present from him, via my estranged husband, but no visit or telephone call. That hurts.

I hope my story will give hope to other mothers. In under a year, things did change. Everyone told me, "Give them time and they'll come round". In my case, it's true. I still have to give my eldest son time. I'm fortunate than most: at least I do have contact. Never give up. I am getting engaged on Christmas Day and my divorce will be final in January 1999. Once my partner's divorce is through, we will marry. I wonder who'll be at the wedding?

PARTING AS FRIENDS

"In recent years mediation has been recognised as an effective means of reducing conflict at the time of divorce. It has not, however, been shown to be successful in facilitating long-term co-parenting. It has not been set up to deal with the complicated social network, interpersonal factors, and interactional dynamics that characterise high-conflict divorce. Nor has mediation been employed as a means to protect the children from long-term divorce issues."

Caught in the Middle: Protecting the children of High-Conflict Divorce
Carla B. Garrity, Mitchell A. Baris

Post-divorce suffering can be agonising and lengthy: everyone knows someone who has been distressed by its prolonged misery. Divorce and its unhappy effects are not an uncommon experience for most of us within our families or social circles. Yet although not unusual, it still carries a stigma particularly among affected children who feel a variety of emotions: shame, humiliation, embarrassment, guilt, fear, anger. It is particularly harrowing when a relationship with children breaks up in such a brutal way one can almost feel the children's pain.

In Dinosaurs Divorce: A Guide for Changing Families, a picture-sequence book on explaining divorce to very young children, Laurene Krasny Brown and Marc Brown describe the very early stages of some children's potential reactions in the chapter, Feeling Upset:

"When parents split up children often have different feelings: Ben is sad. Zoe is angry. Clare feels afraid. Luke is confused. Harry is ashamed. Jo feels guilty. Beth is relieved. Sam is worried."

Debate must begin now for our children's sake on re-defining our reactions to splitting up a family and divorce in the 21st Century. It is so common it should begin to be tolerably acceptable both to children and adults, provided it is handled not only with great sensitivity but with a deep awareness of the significance of both parents being equally committed to limiting emotional damage to their children. Both parents should continue to share equally in their children's future lives.

But divorce today, despite being increasingly common, is still perceived as a bereavement and still continues to give great pain to all at its centre for a very long time. It is frequently quoted as a well-known but hackneyed litany as being one of the three major causes of severe stress along with house-moving and actual bereavement. But divorce is now so widespread, particularly in the United States, that what might be described as a sector of commerce has been set up, almost without people acknowledging it. Divorced people are supported through counselling, courses, books, support agencies and a myriad of other means including, if people don't want face-to-face contact, audio cassettes.

Bill Ferguson, a former divorce attorney has "showed his clients how to end the cycle of conflict and restore love" by broadcasting his advice on tape,

How to Divorce as Friends (4 Audio Cassettes Running Time: 110 Minutes):

> *"You can divorce as friends! No matter how painful or destructive your relationship is today, you have the ability to turn your situation around. You can end the conflict and restore the love, one human being to another. Sound impossible? Well it's not! It can happen for you. These four audio-cassettes show, step by step, how to end conflict and restore co-operation in even the most difficult relationships. You will learn how to heal hurt, and be free of guilt and resentment. You will discover how to resolve issues quickly and effortlessly. You will learn how to part as friends."*

Divorce Source Inc., USA describe his success:

> *"Fifteen percent of his clients never divorced, and the ones who did were able to do so as friends. His work has been featured in newspapers, magazines, radio and television shows across the country, including The Oprah Winfrey Show."*

Public debate of divorce in our society and its devastating legacy for ill-prepared children and adults alike, together with public acceptance of its negative as well as its positive aspects, is long, long overdue. Like the overhauling of an antiquated political party or a large old-fashioned organisation which persists in wilfully ignoring the public's wishes for it to transform and discard out-dated, irrelevant dogma in the process, we must begin to accept it.

After prolific media examples exposing The Full Monty collapse of the marriages or long-term partnerships of both very public and very private people – and in such explicit detail we almost feel qualified to express opinions – when will society begin to accept that unsuccessful relationships are like broken cars, teeth, lawn mowers, washing machines or business ventures. These fall apart or break down for a combination of ordinary, mundane reasons to do with over-use, over-work or the wrong combination of use and users. Divorce does not need a punishing, expensive campaign of lengthy retribution which impacts forever on our children and on their continuing life-time relationships with both parents.

- Could we accept failed relationships as a ordinary common frailty shared with millions of others?
- Could we redefine marriage in the New Millennium as a working partnership for two level-headed, tolerant, fair-minded people having fairly equal measures of competence and incompetence, sense and stupidity, having the foresight to reach understandings about each other's wide and far-ranging differences which might include phobias, crazy hobbies or dislike of each other's in-laws?
- Could we re-explore the foundation of two lives joined together in which two people, heavily committed to each other and to each other's success, perhaps rejecting the crass vulgarity of 20th century wedding preparation trash, try to find out with real seriousness before the marriage and with the help of professionals, if each is right for the other?
- Could we equally accept, if our particular system of marriage entered into with honesty and integrity at the very beginning does eventually fail, we are not failures ourselves?
- Could we give up a burning need for revenge, vindication and redress through our children, possessions or the legal system?
- Could we accept it is only the relationship which has failed, not we ourselves?
- Could we ever consider the sensible possibility of marriage contracts lasting 10, 15, 20 years or so and then reviewing them?
- Could we consider that divorce in the 21st Century might one day be socially acceptable and even thought of as a welcome break in a marriage

contract, *provided* always the ending of a marriage with children has the interests of those children uppermost?

• Could we use our understanding and experiences of life to accept that marriage is not the beginning of a fairytale and divorce is not the end of life? Divorce may, initially, seem like a kind of death, parting with dreams and expectations especially if one has tried hard.

• Could we ever begin to accept that divorce simply marks the end of one part of our life and the beginning of another?

• Could all these concepts be passed on, from one generation to another, so that our children in future are not irreparably damaged throughout their lives but see themselves as a continuing part of their parents' union which has had to be re-formed.

• Could all family members, mother, father, children, extended family continue to belong to each other in a Family Union?

• Could we accept, as normal, that divorced parents share their children's lives in separate homes wherever possible?

Douglas Darnall, a licensed psychologist and Chief Executive Officer of PsyCare, an outpatient psychology center in Youngstown, Ohio, USA, teaches workshops and parental alienation syndrome and divorce to mental health care professionals. In his book, Divorce Casualties: Protecting Your Children from Parental Alienation, a guide for divorced parents to help them understand the effects of their actions on their children, he believes that:

> *"Some parents consciously, blatantly, and even maliciously harm their ex-spouse through negative comments and actions. Others simply sigh or tense up at the mention of the other parent, causing guilt and anxiety in the children. The result is a child full of hate, fear, and rejection toward an unknowing and often undeserving parent....[Such] behaviours, whether conscious or unconscious, could evoke a disturbance in the relationship between a child and the other parent."*

Relate, the couple counselling charity in the United Kingdom has undertaken research, as well as a number of initiatives, to meet the demands of marriage breakdown. In commenting upon one area of research, Sarah Bowler, the Chief Executive of Relate says

> *"...Relate counselling also assists some couples to part with less acrimony*

which is essential for the welfare of those children involved in parental separation. The continuing insecurity in family life in the UK has ensured a demand and interest in the services Relate provides. Relate intends to use the findings of this research to build on, extend and improve its counselling services in the future."

She goes on:

"Already, over the last year [1998] Relate has launched a number of new services to meet the changing needs of couples as they approach the Millennium. They are

- A highly successful telephone counselling service, 'Relate-line'.
- A single session service, entitled 'Consultation with a Counsellor'. Practical and solution focused, this service aims to help Relate clients find a way through their present relationship difficulties.
- A marriage preparation programme entitled 'Couples'. This course enables couples considering marriage, or a committed relationship, to learn negotiation and conflict management skills. These vital skills can prevent relationship breakdown and help couples to enjoy their relationship to the full.
- A support service entitled 'New Life, New Challenge' for people going through with separation and divorce.

Pat Krantzler, the director of Creative Divorce, Love & Marriage Counselling Center, San Francisco, California, is the author of The New Creative Divorce:

"millions of divorced men and women achieve happier lives during and after their divorce. In The New Creative Divorce, Dr. Krantzler shows you how to turn your personal pain into positive growth, including specific advice on how to:

- Move beyond blaming your ex-spouse to focusing on the positive changes you can make.
- Discover what went wrong in your marriage and not make the same mistakes again.
- Tell when and whether you're ready for a new relationship.
- Maintain a strong bond with your children.

• Develop a healthy approach to new sexual relationships

The New Creative Divorce shows you how to make your divorce a positive and creative part of your life. It is profoundly realistic and hopeful, and gives you the advice, reassurance, and direction you need to build the life you want during and after your divorce."

After all these examples of people working in a burgeoning and a profitable divorce industry, society in all parts of the Western world must begin to accept that separation, splitting up, divorce and re-marriage is statistically inevitable and a pattern of modern life and that we must learn to adapt to accept this.

Many people today continue to form families in relationships which are inadequately and poorly prepared. It is perhaps human nature that we will continue to go into a relationship with our hearts first rather than our heads. No one goes into a relationship knowing it is going to break up but, statistically viewed, that is an expensive mistake.

Constructing a family framework in the future whether in a formal marriage or not should be attempted with a clear heart and a clear head if it is to achieve any degree of long-term permanence and success. For the sake of our children this is critically and vitally important for the stability of their lives.

DIANE'S STORY

I left my husband after 24 years of marriage and my two daughters, 18 and 22.

Although they both knew the marriage was over, when I met M. and decided to leave, their attitude changed. For the first few weeks, they would only speak to me on the phone and then the crunch came when my eldest daughter called me a slut and said they did not want anything more to do with me. My youngest daughter phoned me and said I was not fit to be called a mother and my cards and letters were returned with abuse written on them.

I, like you, have resigned myself to not having any contact with them. Although they still live in the matrimonial home with my ex-husband, I decided to move away. Although, like you, I am happy with my life and have no regrets, I do miss them.

People do not understand how hurtful it is and not many people understand our children's attitude especially when you have been a good mother.

I think this is what makes up cope – knowing we were good mothers.

It gave me great comfort knowing I was not the only one in this situation.

Mend It or End It?

I tried too hard. I wanted the children to have a secure family life, home-cooked nutritional food, good moral standards, and sociable behaviour, clean clothes and happily-married parents. I had to wear a mask to carry on the burden of an unhappy marriage. Trying to carry on caring drained me and made me bad-tempered at times. It is easy to see how my children have judged me as an awful mother.

This is not self-flagellation but accuracy. Of course there were countless times when I kissed, cuddled or hugged them – I remember some: snuggling on the couch, dancing around the room with my youngest son, me jiving in a sad, old-fogey way before he reached the age of being judgmental. Sitting in the front passenger seat on a long journey, on the times when we did have a company car, stretching out my arms behind me in the car, so the twins could have one hand each to hold on a 2-hour journey strapped in their seats, giving in to my second son's pleas for pet mice, dogs.

But the effect of being married to someone who has manners, behaviour and character which are the opposite of one's own is that one instinctively looks for these negative characteristics mirrored in the children, knowing how unattractive they are to society.

If I have learnt anything in the last 25 years of having been married to someone who was finally responsible for ending my life as a mother, it is that I know now, with absolute clarity, how tempting it is to view life as worthless when parenthood ends in the way mine did.

Life seemed pointless and empty when energies invested with such intensity into mothering life are eventually perceived as worthless by your own children. Suicide seemed to welcome me with open arms and it is easy to see why many parents in my situation have succumbed. If you live for your children, life without them seems pointless, barren and meaningless. Life only had meaning for me if my children were in it. To some extent that still holds true. I hold suicide at bay, but it is now a distant dot on the horizon, not a near landmark.

If only we could teach young people preparing for a life together that marriage is, potentially, a survival course in barren land and a blind walk through a minefield. If only we could teach young people preparing to be parents that babies and children can dramatically alter the dynamics in a relationship.

Living together with children whether married or not, is a testing ground to see if we are willing to adapt to each other's dissimilar, diverse characteristics or opinions. Family life is not a theme park containing pleasure rides of thrills and spills but a potential battlefield unless we are generously co-operative from the beginning in a balanced, mutually supportive relationship. Most of all, we need to survive the disappointment of being disillusioned about each other and give up pretensions about ourselves.

In The Relate Guide to Better Relationships, Sarah Litvinoff talks about the hope that some couples have – or it may be truer to say one half of the couple – that marriage may improve the relationship if it is rocky:

"Couples who are not getting on well together sometimes hope that making it legal will help. This is often the case if one of you wants to marry more than the other and it is causing friction between you. But while one of you might feel more secure after the wedding the other might equally feel more trapped, causing a different set of problems.

This also happens when one of you feels the other slipping away. Offering marriage at this time can help temporarily but the reasons that caused you to draw apart are likely to remain. You must be sure in your own minds that the problems you are experiencing as a couple before marriage can be sorted out between you and not expect the wedding alone to make them go away."

Marriage or living together is a ceaselessly strenuous assault course testing our ability to take on new skills, particularly when children enter the scene. From then onwards we are on trial, being tested and examined continuously to see how strong, adaptable and unified we really are, both as a parent and as a spouse within our marriage, and whether we can adjust to unique sometimes arduous situations in shifting sand.

Love is the start of things. Absence of it is the beginning of the end. You don't just stop loving someone overnight. It takes time for love to fade, dying slowly while day-to-day life goes on. It is seldom killed outright by one single act although it can happen to some like that. Attitudes to children, in-laws, extended family, illness, morals, work, humour, manners, energy, social graces, personal habits, hobbies, interests all affect love and esteem for one's partner.

Sometimes it can be one incident and one will watch hawk-like for a repeat of it and so it builds up over years. Each incident becomes a brick which is built up, layer by layer, until one day you're standing in front of an edifice of disillusionment with the sudden realisation the person you remember marrying has vanished.

You may not stop liking the person you're living with but you stop loving them and wanting to share your life with them. If the differences seem, after some while, so diametrically opposed to you and your way of thinking and living, its effect can be catastrophic for the marriage.

People change with maturity, adapting to changes in circumstances, responsibilities or to children, illness, further education, redundancy, bereavement. One of you may have had experiences in child-rearing, the workplace, ill-health or in caring for physically ill or mentally disabled children or come into close contact with special people, some of which may have had a profound effect on changing you fundamentally.

One partner may not be sympathetic to these changes or may not notice or indeed care that the other attaches great importance to matters which he/she considers unimportant.

You may have met someone, not necessarily a future partner, who has influenced your thinking, you may have travelled in the past, taken up physical exercise or a hobby recently, perhaps adopted an interest or voluntary work which takes up more time, or returned to further education as a mature student or paid work as an employee.

Whatever has happened to affect you, you may now have a much wider, far-ranging view of the world than you had formerly, making you think more deeply than before.

If one partner is not sympathetic to the other changing partner it may be he/she is jealous or confused at the changes, perhaps feels left behind. You may be accused of forgetting your roots, being big-headed, wasting time. You may start to have more arguments which are not only escalating in heat but increasing in number.

Relate conducted a survey on arguments, (published on 12 February 1998 with Candis magazine) to coincide with the publication of its new book, Stop Arguing, Start Talking . Its findings, admittedly with just a small sample of the population (over 2,000 men and women having filled out an extensive questionnaire on their personal argument styles and topics), revealed just one part of the whole story of what really happens when couples argue:

- More than a third of respondents argue more than once a week. Couples aged 18-34 with children aged 0-4 are the ones who argue most.
- Those whose household income is £10,000 or less are twice as likely to argue daily than those whose household income is £20,000 or over.
- Money rates as the top argument topic, followed by personal habits, children, housework, sex, work, parents and friends.
- Half of arguments take place in the evenings. 26 per cent argue at weekends, while 23 per cent argue before a special event. The most common argument pattern is a fast and furious row, followed by no communication. Other patterns include shouting matches, bickering and exchanges of accusations. As well as arguing in the home, couples argue in bed, while travelling and on holiday.

Most respondents felt arguments only 'sometimes' resolved problems in their relationships. Thirty-nine per cent felt they resolved arguments 'by talking over their concerns'. Others were likely to 'sweep the subject under the carpet' or 'have one person apologise to the other'.

The survey went on to summarise what people argue about:

"**Money**
Most money arguments are over spending priorities.
Low-income groups are more than twice as likely to argue over money issues than higher income groups.

Sex

Men (23 per cent) are more likely than women (13 per cent) to argue about lack of foreplay in sex.

Two-thirds of women who argue about sex argue about how often they make love.

79 per cent of respondents who earn £20,000+ argue about frequency of sex. 20 per cent of the same group feel their sex lives lack imagination and experimentation.

Personal Habits

Well over half of couples see untidiness as an annoying personal habit.

Work

Those who earn more than £20,000 are more likely to argue over too much time spent at work, and too much time spent talking about work, than those in lower income brackets.

Housework

Arguments over housework are common. Two-thirds of women respondents say men do too little housework and male respondents agree.

Parents

Half of those who argue about parents do so because they feel their parents interfere.

Friends

40 per cent of arguments over friends arise because of a partner's behaviour in front of friends."

This small survey illustrates some of the stresses and tensions some couples encounter every day. The findings confirm that many couples cope with their arguments. For those who don't, talking to a Relate counsellor can help them discover what lies behind their rows and bickering.

Talking, talking and yet more talking can help whether it is talking to a counsellor either separately or jointly with your partner. But it is far more important to talk to your partner. Listening, though, can be the most difficult part for both of you.

Going often to play at a friend's house in the late 1950s when I was about 8 or 9, I was struck by an unusual quietness in her home which I could not, at such a young age, either understand or put into words. There were notes all over the place, propped up against tins, stuck on doors, lying on the table. Much later, I discovered that, many years previously, my friend's parents had stopped talking to each other. They only communicated by note. Her father, a particularly reticent, reserved man, had regular fits of worry or depression, feeling compelled to remind his wife to close doors, turn off taps and close jar lids tightly. Only they had stopped speaking. (A friend also told me her grandparents conversed only through the housekeeper.)

The findings undertaken by Relate and other similar research by social policy groups will only confirm what most people already know from personal experience in their own marriage or second-hand knowledge of the difficulties in marriages or relationships of others. It is extremely difficult living with someone who seems to have contrasting or opposing ideas on how to share a home, a marriage, children and who seems oblivious most of the time to the need to meet a partner half-way in adapting to continually changing life experiences.

OTHER AREAS OF DISPUTE

- One partner has serious priorities, perhaps the children's education and upbringing – the other places less importance on them.
- One become accomplished in some skilled area at work or at home – the other accuses him/her of neglecting the family but really means himself/herself.
- One wants to socialise or party – the other wants to stay home, watch TV.
- One wants encouragement and some attention paid to the trouble being taken in self-development – the other is either scathingly critical or becomes withdrawn.

Changes for your partner might not be realistic an option for the moment but you might have tried to change yourself and your own attitude to him/her. You might have decided that it is best to ignore the things which have disturbed, offended, upset or frightened you but there comes a point when you feel you can no longer do so or you no longer want to.

Perhaps the point has been reached when you feel, "enough is enough" when it affects your sanity, keeping you confined in a stiflingly narrow world or perhaps the point has been reached when you suspect you and/or the children might be in danger of becoming either physically or mentally abused or both.

It's a familiar argument, although a simplistic one, and one part of Relate's research seems to bear it out, that some quarrels in a failing marriage seem to be mainly about two things: sex and money.

Too much or too little of one may bring a row to a head but the underlying causes of marriage breakdown are usually far more complex. Lying just under the surface, the real reasons for failings in a marriage may sometimes be brought to a head by sex or money problems in a heated row. The actual reasons may be buried too deep and are seldom articulated rationally and logically.

Sarah Litvinoff's chapter on Communication (The Relate Guide to Better Relationships) deals with listening and hearing techniques and the way in which one partner will 'block' the other:

> *"Blocking what your partner says is an effective technique for avoiding listening. The harder a subject is for your partner to talk about, the easier it is to shut him or her up by criticising, sounding shocked, correcting, laughing, changing the subject, arguing, weeping, shouting or any other ploy you can think of rather than listening. Talking about difficult and emotional matters takes courage and needs a sympathetic listener. Without this it seems safer to give up trying."*

To put one reason for wanting to mend or end your marriage into calm, controlled language using the right occasion is difficult enough. To have to express a list of reasons which would adequately explain to the other partner just what is wrong, and to choose the right time to say it, is almost impossible.

To explain or clarify those frustrations to a partner who truly doesn't understand or wilfully won't can be a frustrating, losing battle. Trying to justify yourself at the wrong moment can result in a jumble of confusion which may lead to yet more arguments, feelings of failure or defeat.

When my older children were 6 and 8 and the twins were about 6 months old, I remember sitting on the second stair in our large Victorian house (it had 42 stairs to the top). I was crying, holding a baby in each arm. Their father walked in from work, looked at me and asked what was wrong.

He had recently completed a two-week course on Effective Public Speaking for the executives in his company and had been high on the adrenaline it had given him in offering yet another platform to show off his articulacy skills. I was lethargically weak with tiredness, partly to do with having looked after him and all four children the previous month after their bout of chickenpox all within a fortnight of each other. The twins at 5 months had suffered particularly badly, as had he.

I tried, incoherently, to explain.

"For God's sake, woman, stop being so bloody dramatic and explain exactly what's wrong!"

It was as if cold water had been thrown in my face. It cleared my mind so I could focus on just four things which had been particularly bothering me.

"I suppose what I'm trying to tell you is that you never feed the cat or put the rubbish out, you're never here and you're a bloody lousy husband."

He looked at me pityingly, and walked away.

Designing a Family

Some women thinking of marrying or living together today, even in this climate of self-sufficiency, independence and equality of earning power, still have some notion at the back of their minds their husband will take care of them financially and they can give up their job or leave their education incomplete.

When their marriage starts to go wrong, they feel trapped without their own security of financial liberty, and realise how vital it is to have completed some training, special skills or further education which can be built on to give them their own independence and self-esteem. This can then contribute to all the other issues going wrong in a failing marriage or relationship, exacerbating feelings and tensions, diminishing their self-confidence rapidly. If they have children at this point women are caught in a dead-end for what seems to be a very long time.

We could all write books about why our marriage or relationship is breaking down, has broken down or shows all the signs of being about to break down. But the reasons we get married or want to live together, are not usually why we try to stay married or committed. Time alters that earlier vision of a life planned together when viewed from a romanticised courtship without the strain of children or money worries.

Financial tensions, shared possessions, a shared house or mortgage but most of all shared children, contribute to just some of the reasons marriages last long after all communication has broken down between that original romantic courting couple.

If there were equality of opportunities for earning power, equality of money in an equal partnership from the beginning in an equally shared house dividing domestic chores and the care of children, marriages might still end. But would we have gone into that marriage in the first place?

How many women today earning their own money and able to support themselves financially would be willingly courted and married at an early age?

How many young, working women today put off getting married because there is no need to escape from home? With financial security, development of personal maturity established at their own pace in their chosen and secure home environment, they have time to wait for marriage until they are really sure.

Some may even choose or prefer to have children while remaining single mothers not committed to any tied relationship, and may continue to work to be self-supporting.

How many older mothers today, who married one or several decades ago really got married at an age when they felt ready, or simply married to escape from home or a drab working environment?

How many of those mothers fell pregnant during a relationship which had not perhaps fully developed but nevertheless felt pressured to get married?

How many had a strong, natural biological urge for children and felt they needed to marry someone as a secondary issue, someone with whom at the time they believed they could spend the rest of their lives?

Whatever the answers and whoever falls into the various bands of statistics, the undisputed fact remains that the divorce figures, whilst declining somewhat, are still extremely high and have a damaging effect on children. Even without the formality of marriage, partnerships with children and common-law marriages with children continue to break up and new households with diverse groups of parent/children relationships are formed with varied-aged children of assorted parental backgrounds. This remains an undeniable part of our modern society, affecting all areas of the population regardless of wealth or poverty.

We are not a society where there is yet equal earning power or shared child care. We hear of fathers who are house husbands while the wife goes to work. They are the exception which is why they feature, usually in women's magazines. One reads of women who are mothers in powerful positions earning huge sums.

They too are the exception, which is why we get to hear about them. They can arrange their lives smoothly with the luxury of money as well as disarrange their lives with equal ease. Who can say whether there is less damage inflicted on their children after separation or divorce than on the children of divorced or separated people living on the breadline?

People will continue to co-habit or marry, people will continue to divorce and sometimes re-marry.

Most of us readily and happily take the responsibility for having created our children within a loving family network. We are eager and willing to accept that it remains our parental duty, as well as our natural inclination to want to continue nurturing our children within a loving family setting, however radically changed that structure becomes.

The Stepfamily Network Inc. of the United States believes that

> *"We are recreating the design of family faster than we are creating language, behaviour, expectations and responsibilities."*

Some of the associations for step-families included in their network across the world include names which register the shifts and variations in today's society: Center for Changing Families, Center for the Family in Transition, Stepmothers International Inc., Step by Step: Helping Stepfamilies in South Australia, Canadian Stepfamily Association, The Second Wives Club, National Stepfamily Association UK. Their common ethos acknowledges that change in one family has taken place and, in so doing, emphasises the positive aspects of not only accepting that new family but of adapting to that new family's diverse and unique environment.

Encouragement and support is offered across a wide spectrum so the new family can not only begin to build a new, healthy framework but can actually strengthen it.

• Could we begin to accept new ideas on the un-doing of our marriage if it is not working?

• Could we begin now to discuss, openly and intelligently with our partner, the practical issues, *for our children*, of separation and divorce?

• Could we allow children the freedom of 'belonging' to both parents in separate homes and keeping in close, friendly, contact with estranged partners ourselves, for the sake of the children?

In her book Family Transformation Through Divorce and Remarriage: A Systemic Approach, (Routledge, London, 1999), Margaret Robinson estimates that one in eight families is probably a stepfamily:

"Many of the children of these families will be referred to child and family guidance clinics with divorce-related problems, while others, whose parent(s) are often living near the poverty line, may be considered to be seriously at risk through neglect or abuse. The past twenty years have seen the emergence of family therapy, as well as the development of family research, some of it related to divorce, stepfamilies and the effects of divorce on children."

Her book looks at:

"the complete divorce-remarriage-stepfamily cycle in the context of the demographic data, the legal processes and the systemic theoretical framework. For each phase of the cycle, the author describes the stages of development, summarises the relevant research and illustrates the effects on family members with case examples. In doing so, she discusses the various ways of intervening with families during the divorce process and the differing orientations of the professionals involved. In the last phase of the cycle, she introduces the concept of the 'good enough' post-divorce and remarried family, attempting to define it and provide appropriate guidelines for families and practitioners. Finally, she outlines some of the present research proposals which are likely to change both attitudes and practice in relation to families during divorce." [extract from Routledge publicity]

Marriage, divorce and re-marriage will, statistically, be a continuing part of our children's future lives. Society in general but divorcing parents in particular must undergo a vigorous transformation of out-dated attitudes towards divorce whereby children suffer immeasurably for the 'sins' of one parent.

The new century should witness a renaissance of thinking and, in so doing, revitalise the family unit. Society must accept that many children will enter far wider multi-family groupings in the future. A 'normal' cycle of life for one in three families may mean a process of much change involving separations, splitting-ups and re-forming of disparate family units, not always enshrined in a marriage contract.

But the two parents who produced the child are the child's 'family' for life, and for the duration of that child's life, not just for the duration of the marriage or living-together of his/her parents.

Parents creating a stepfamily must maintain the old destroyed family in another form, perhaps called The Family Union. All parents should strive to maintain friendly links with important adults in the child's life. Members of the new step-family as well as the old family have a continuing moral obligation to encourage and allow all children belonging to a miscellany of blood parents to continue to share in the lives of those parents.

But more crucially, parents must quickly learn to bury divorce or separation-related issues linked to either partner and recognise their lifelong responsibility for encouraging their child's continuing bonds within the old family to be fostered without ill-will. Family life, albeit in an altered format, must continue for the sake of the children.

While a step-family is being created, the old family must be re-created. Children have much to teach their parents in learning to accept this simple concept.

Patti's Story

I was divorced in 1986 when my daughter was 8 years old. In 1990 I married a man who has two children. My husband also has an ex-wife, ex in-laws, plus my husband's ex-wife has a long time partner. The coming together of my daughter and myself, my husband, his children, his ex-wife, her partner and her parents has been a very difficult task.

Our children were young teenagers when we met. They seemed to bond with relative ease, especially our daughters who are the same age. My stepson and daughter always seemed to have an understanding with one another. Of course there were fights, as in any sibling relationship but they knew from the very beginning that we were a family and that this family was "Until death do us part."

Today our children are 21 and 23, beginning their own lives but they still share a sense of family. It was hardest for the adults to accept and live peacefully with all of the new players. I am happy and proud to say we are now an extended family and are continually learning how to interpret the roles we have in each other's lives. Once we made the concerted effort to acknowledge and create this new form of family, we have done so with ease.

It is very difficult to form a blending and extended family. Part of the dilemma of blending families is that there are few, if any, cultural guidelines to follow. For example, we know how to behave and what is expected of us when we become in-laws. But we do not really know what our role is with our spouse's ex-spouse. There is no language for these new members of the family and, for the most part, we do not acknowledge them as members of our extended family, nor do we think of them as friends. They may actually be seen as adversaries, intruders and a relationship built on this type of foundation can be very draining. Without guidelines and language it is very difficult to create family or friendships.

It is now almost two years since we have established an understanding that we are in each other's lives and that we can be supportive to one another. We can even be friends. My own story is probably not all that different from the many other women who have married men who have previously been married. It took over eight years for the adults to come together. The most difficult part of my journey was learning how to be friends with my husband's ex-wife, Jane. It was something I had to do, not for the sake of my husband or his children, but for my own well-being. I knew, too, that it would take time and patience.

For the first seven years of my marriage my husband's relationship with Jane was based on anger and fighting. I had to step away and give them space to heal their wounds. Perhaps, too, I was jealous of their relationship, past and present. I think all three of us, really, had no idea of how to behave. The difficulties between the three of us kept growing and none of us were capable, at the time, to make the necessary adjustments. After a year of turmoil and confusion, I sent her a note asking to simply put the past aside and to begin again as friends. I give Jane much credit because she has been able to do this with such dignity.

Jane's father died recently and it was our privilege to help support the grieving family which of course included my stepchildren, their mother and grandmother.

Having been able to succeed at this relationship has been, and continues to be, a very gratifying and healing experience.

(from Stepfamily Network Inc., USA: One Family's Journey to Healing, http://www.stepfamily.net/articleo1.htm)

STEP FAMILIES WITHIN THE FAMILY UNI

My second husband had a friend who had been divorced and who afterwards married a woman who had, herself, been married before. This friend used to talk about the various children in their family as being, "mine, her's and our's."

ChildLine offer the following statistics on the modern changed family:

- Forecasts suggest that the number of step families will continue to grow, with increasing numbers of children spending some of their childhood in a one-parent household. Currently, about 1 in 10 children currently live with one natural parent and one step-parent.
- Only 40% of the population consist of a married couple with dependent children, compared to 52% in 1961, although this situation is still the most common experience for 7 in 10 young people.
- Divorce now ends one in two new marriages, with two out of every three re-marriages failing. 25% of children will now see their parents divorce.

ChildLine believes that

"many children, living in a variety of family environments during their childhood and adolescence, are affected by changes in the family today. In 1994/5 over 10,000 children called ChildLine to talk about their family relationships, many of which concerned step-families. Some children are very happy but for others, coping with step-parents, step-brothers and step-sisters can be a difficult and lonely experience."

ChildLine offers distressed children an opportunity to talk about their anger or their grief:

"It can be hard to find someone with the time to listen when so many changes are happening and children sometimes feel that they are expected just to get on with it. Although things won't be the same, there can be many positive things about being part of a stepfamily and that when things go wrong, there may be ways to put them right again. Young people may need to go through a grieving process, letting old habits, family ceremonies and

ways of doing things go by. They can feel a lot of stress, anger and sadness. Talking can help with all these feelings."

What children have told ChildLine counsellors about being part of a step-family:

"Michael, 12: "It's hard getting to know lots of new people all at once."
Alison, 15: "He seems to think he can tell me what to do, but he hasn't got the right. He isn't my real dad."
Janine, 13: "I feel like mum's a different person."
Remi, 13: "I think that Samuel and his children are more special to her now."
Alice, 15: "It feels wrong when I'm having fun with dad and his new wife, when I think of mum by herself."
Stef, 13: "I'm not sure who to go to now, when I want to talk about things."
Paula, 10: "I most want my mum back and for everything to be OK again."
Alex, 16: "Every time I go out with dad, he quizzes me about mum and my new step dad. I feel like a spy."

Life is complicated and all family life is deeply complex particularly in split families. If children are going to be part of a stepfamily, there is a real danger; in the joy of beginning a new relationship between two loving people, of overlooking the many pitfalls posing a potential risk to your children's well-being in their efforts to adapt to their new family.

If your children feel isolated or threatened by your new relationship, the risks of endangering new-found unity with your new partner are very real. To repeat the earlier statistic: two out of every three re-marriages fail. It is difficult not to draw certain conclusions that poor preparation for a family life with someone's else children within the second marriage could have created insurmountable difficulties.

Christopher Compston, a divorce barrister and judge for 33 years and who himself experienced the divorce of his own parents as a child, later having two step-fathers and who, much later as an adult, became divorced himself, discusses the effects on children and stepchildren of a new relationship for their parents in, Breaking up without cracking up:

"Remember that one of the main causes of failure or difficulty in new relationships is the effect of the children. Children almost always remain

loyal to their own parents and will, time and time again, cause trouble for step-parents. It is only natural for us to feel closer to our own children than to others. If you are going to set up a home, both of you bringing children to the family, there may well be conflicts of loyalty. These conflicts can be resolved but it is glib thinking not to anticipate them before you embark on a new relationship."

The step-children might not be the root cause of the final problem but their emotional difficulties in coming to terms with the ending of their own parents' marriage might have caused behavioural problems. If these not have been recognised or supported by wise parents as well as wise step-parents, in certain cases these may have contributed to some of the reasons for the second marriage failing.

Are you prepared, for the sake of all the children, to sustain old relationships within the new family you are creating? Are you happy for your new partner to see his/her former wife/husband on a regular basis for the sake of your new step-children and so they can establish their own forms of Family Union?

How willing would you be to work with your former partner to maintain links and friendship, for the sake of your children?

CareZone, a Dawn Project supporting children and their families in coming to terms with their new lives apart, offer an e-mail service by which children can contact them if they are distressed. ShareZone is the problem page for children in which they invite children to share their problems if the family has been affected by divorce or separation:.

> *"You can e-mail us or write to us about your problems and, if you want to, you can have your letter published on this page. You need not use your real name, just make up a name if you like. You can reply to problems you see on this page, too. If you have good advice or help to offer we will publish it here, because someone somewhere is having the same sort of problems as you!*

> After my dad moved out, my little brother started wetting the bed again. I find it hard to pay attention at school and last week I got into a fight with someone, about nothing really. I'm worried that things will never ever feel right again."

The reply to Paul:

"When there is a split-up in the family, you are bound to feel a lot of intense emotions – e.g. anger and especially a strong sense of loss of your Dad.

You will need support for yourself. Is there someone you can tell what has happened and how you feel? If not, try writing your feelings down, on paper. But you will need to give yourself time to start feeling right again. If you have thought of anything else that might help Paul, or if you have had similar problems or feelings, e-mail us and we will put your response in ShareZone."

Other e-mails from children on the ShareZone website include the following:

"My stepfather is always shouting at me and finding fault with what I do or say. When I'm wearing my nightie or pyjamas, I don't like the way he looks at me. It makes me feel uncomfortable. What should I do?

When dad comes to the house to collect me for the weekend he and mum always argue about money. I feel unhappy all weekend after that and dad gets angry. I don't know what to do about it.

My step mum always lets her children get away with things but with me and my sister she is very strict. When I said it wasn't fair she said she treated us all the same. This just isn't true."

How ready are you to admit that some of these children and their problems might be reflected in your new family environment and that maintaining good relationships will be difficult, but vital, for the sake of all the children? If all the children are happy and settled, and know that all parents are openly and positively encouraging them to retain links with both biological parents, grandparents and other important family members it surely follows that the whole family will be more settled and happier.

If there is unhappiness among children because their needs have not been recognised, you will need the skill of a magician to juggle complicated issues as well as the stamina of an athlete to sustain changing and diverse relationships across a dissimilar range of personalities who are also trying to adapt.

The National Stepfamily Association which supports people in changing families estimate that 18 million children and adults are involved in stepfamily relationships in the UK. They believe that

> *"Stepfamilies represent a re-investment. We are determined to spread the word about just how resourceful people often are on a daily basis when they are committed to building families and creating environments in which everyone can flourish. This will encourage other stepfamilies as they try to do their best in the midst of change."*

The National Stepfamily Association provide information and support across a wide range of issues and worries:

"My new partner has never had children and doesn't know how to be a father."

"Once their new baby arrives he won't want to be my dad."

"The children return from access visits like wild things – what can we do?"

"How can we be a 'real' family when the children still visit their dad?"

"My experience of step-parenting is that it is singularly the most traumatic and demanding thing I have ever done; nothing prepares you for it."

ChildLine has researched other worries that stepchildren can have within their new family:

> *"Sometimes stepchildren continue to see both their birth parents but others may lose touch with one of them. There can be pressure to be a 'perfect family' but it takes time to get to know one another. Just getting used to different ways that each person has can create problems. Different rules and expectations, kinds of food eaten, when homework is done or what household tasks you would be expected to do are all things that cause stress.*

> *Family holidays, Christmas and other religious festivals are all times when each family has its own way of doing things and it can be hard to adjust to new ways. Children might have to move house, neighbourhood and school. It can mean losing friends and moving away from loved relatives. Families combining can mean less privacy; for example, sharing a*

bedroom, or never having somewhere quiet to do homework or just be alone. It can be a difficult time for parents too – they are having to adjust as well and may be having to be a parent for a child they hardly know."

Whoever and wherever the children's biological parents and step-parents are – and whatever you may think of them – in your own, newly formed household with your new partner, try and make sure that even if there is a varied assortment of "mine, her's and ours," all children feel they still belong to both parents within their own unique Family Union, that they are retaining their links with important adults in their family, particularly grandparents, and that everyone is committed to supporting them in making difficult adjustments in what seems to them an alien, deeply upsetting environment.

Stay friends, even if it is just a surface friendship, with the most important people in the children's lives.

Splitting Up

...research began to show that it was remaining in prolonged disturbed relationships that was more likely to lead to impaired development rather than simply losing a relationship. For example, the discord and emotional conflict surrounding parental divorce was shown to be much more damaging to a child's psychological development than parental death."

Attachment Theory for Social Work Practice, David Howe, School of Health and Social Work, University of East Anglia, Norwich.

Staying in a fragmenting or collapsing relationship causing conflict within the family can be far worse for your children, in some instances, than leaving. But it is the manner of your leaving which is crucially significant for your children's present and future emotional health.

Are you thinking of leaving because you think you've fallen in love with someone else? Is that someone responsible for breaking up your marriage or had it broken down before? Has your spouse or partner just been discovered having an affair or are you having an affair yourself? In Relate's Guide to Better Relationships, Sarah Litvinoff describes an affair as:

"what most people think of as the crisis in a relationship. For many the idea of their partners becoming involved with someone else is their greatest fear. 'Affair' covers a wide range of situations, from the one-night stand to the relationship that lasts for years. Most people think of an affair as a sexual relationship but some people are also disturbed by friendships with an emotional rather than sexual closeness. By 'affair' we mean any relationship with a third person that threatens the existing relationship between a couple. That is to say, even if one of you considers the outside relationship unimportant, it counts if your partner is unhappy about it and it causes you to re-evaluate your relationship.

It is usual to say that if your partner has an affair it will mean the end. In practice, though, the majority of people stay together after the discovery of an affair.

...There is a sense in which the relationship ends even when you stay together successfully and happily. The old relationship that you had has gone forever. If you stay together you are embarking on a relationship that has to be modified so much that it counts as a new one: the affair changes you both and therefore changes the relationship. Because of this counsellors treat an affair like a bereavement: the old relationship has died and needs to be mourned. For the new relationship to proceed healthily, both of you must recognise this, and therefore go through the stages of grief that accompany loss. Of course, some affairs are less important to both of you and the accompanying emotions are less strong. But when it has been a major crisis in your life, you can expect the impact to be greater."

Sometimes a marriage or relationship breaks down without one of the partners having an affair. A crisis can be reached without a third party becoming involved. But an unhappy marriage can fall apart more rapidly when one unhappy partner is emotionally uncommitted, withdrawn or neglected in the old relationship and susceptible to sympathy, kindness, flattery and the appearance of love offered by someone else. Repeating again the statistic in the previous chapter that more second marriages fall apart, how likely is it that you might become one of these statistics? Even if you decide to live together, this is still a kind of marriage commitment. If there are children on either side you will be creating another family framework within a marriage setting.

The reasons for second failed marriages can only be guessed at. Is it because people marry on the rebound from a broken first marriage or need a sanctuary to which they can escape? Is it because second relationships begun with high hopes and higher expectations soon fracture and break down within that newly-formed second partnership because children's needs have been overlooked? As a consequence, has their distress affected their behaviour and contributed to growing tensions which have over-spilled into your new life?

Are you so unhappy you are prepared to go to any lengths to leave your spouse and children to set up another home with someone from the office, a neighbour, or someone you've met at a party who has flattered, admired, supported or consoled you and with whom you imagine you have fallen in love? It may be real love but it may not be.

Is it admiration or romantic love in which you feature attractively in a good light, or is it the kind of love which will endure family traumas and mundane daily routine?

Consider in the cold light of day whether what you really want is just an escape route. All escape routes come at a price. Could you be about to jump from the fat into the frying pan?

- Deal with one problem at a time or you will soon find yourself embroiled in messy issues, leaving you and your family in turmoil and confusion.
- A safe distance of time between resolving one problem before taking on another is sensible. How many problems can you handle at any one period?
- If you believe your marriage or relationship is finished, resolve this with your partner and the children first, using professionals to pilot, guide and support you.
- If you believe you are in love with someone else, take time to consider this. Take time to get to know that someone as a friend. Try to look at that someone from a distance, not through rose-tinted spectacles. You never truly know someone unless you live with them for a time. How will you manage this?
- If you really are resolved in your decision to want to end your marriage, think about whether you could live by yourself for while. Don't rush. Settle the children into your new life, even if they are still living in the family home, and don't think about bringing anyone else in at this stage. Only you will know how much time you need to judge whether the single life is the one for you for the immediate future and whether you absolutely require that new "someone" in your new life.
- How necessary is that someone to your happiness and well-being away from your old home and your children? How will that someone fit in with your children's lives?
- If you do go, and if you really can't live without, what you truly believe to be, the new love in your life, leave a sensible interval of time, and after you actually believe the children are becoming used to the separate lives their parents are now living, before taking your estranged partner into your confidence.
- Try to explain at some length to your estranged partner that you would like the children to get used to the idea of someone else in your life.
- Introduce new ideas or people very, very gradually to your children and to your estranged partner so these are not used, by either of you, as fresh occasions to score points, settle old grievances or resurrect jealousies.

This may certainly be idealistic, it is unquestionably going to be slow-going but what, after all, is your rush? You have the rest of your life and you want your children to be part of that life, whether you decide to share it with a new partner or whether you, eventually, decide to live your life alone.

My Parents are Getting Divorced is published by the American Bar Association for people who are experiencing divorce. Several highly respected lawyers have written articles on different related issues which are all brought together. The titles of some of the contents are indicative of issues which cause children great unhappiness and include:

- "What is Divorce?
- My Parents Are Getting a Divorce
- In the Beginning
- Wow, It's Confusing!
- What to Do About Your Feelings
- I Wish…
- How Do Divorces End?
- What is a Lawyer?
- How to Talk to Your Lawyer
- Spending Time with Each Parent
- Worries and What to Do About Them
- Advice for Parents"

Edward Teyber, a child-clinical psychologist, Professor of Psychology and Director of the Community Counselling Center at California State University, specialises in post-divorce family relations. His book, Helping Children Cope With Divorce, has chapters on common areas where children routinely feel most anxiety in the early days of a family splitting up

- "Divorce Causes Separation Anxieties: "if Dad Left, Won't Mom Go Away Too?".
- Children Want to Reunite Their Parents.
- Children Feel Responsible for Divorce
- Parental Conflict and Co-operation.
- Children Need Their Mothers and Fathers
- Custody.
- Mediation and the Courts.

- Loyalty Conflicts.
- Parentification: Turning Children into Adults.
- Child-Rearing Practices.
- Step-Families: Forming New Family Relationships."

Separating parents should be acutely aware and ready to discuss and accept that preparing children for splitting up a family is crucial. Children should be considered the most important members of the family to limit the potential of incalculable emotional damage.

Wide-ranging preparation for splitting up a family is vital, especially when those children are taken from one family and mixed in with another with little thought. It is not enough to offer conciliation as part of the divorce proceedings when many children are the product of unmarried relationships.

It is not enough for authorities or political parties to actively promote their support of a cosy image of a united family as part of an election manifesto. Variations on 'The Family' in many guises will proliferate, unite and, statistically, split up. It is putting our heads in the sand to ignore this. Discussion of splitting up a family and its negative effects on children's place in society should even become part of the school curriculum, at a suitable point, because splitting-up and its wide-ranging effects on society and future parenting will continue to concern you, your entire family network and society in the next century across a broad range of issues. Health promotion agencies should be proactive in putting high on their agenda the emotional health risks to children when a family splits up.

Informal family structures, divorce and re-marriage, legal "ownership" of children through Court Orders should be perceived so differently by society in general in the near future that it will lead to radical changes in safeguarding children's emotional well-being when the family framework changes.

Society must now begin to accept that splitting up or divorce is not like dying, merely the dawning of a new and different life in which the original family, while undergoing modification, is nevertheless recognisable in a altered format.

That same but changing family which is splitting up should continue to function with the blessing of all family members, not just for its collective good but for the sake of all its children, for the benefit of their continuing mental and physical health in their present and future life.

Children should not be treated as custody trophies for one parent. It is archaic and barbaric for society to continue to accept that children are like footballs to be kicked into one net and kept there as a goal for one side's prize-winning score while the losing side looks on and is subsequently relegated.

Irene's Story

I think, until such time as women are financially independent, there will always be problems. I fully agree with one of the points you make about living on your own for a while after you leave. But this is not easy unless you have the ability to support yourself. I had only part-time jobs during my marriage, and most women give up their careers when they have a family.

Children see you only as a mother, which is as it should be, so if it were possible to move out, they could learn to think of you as a person in your own right, with your own needs, faults, etc., not just the overall carer, provider, comforter and everything else a mother has to be.

Like you, I hate the word "divorce". How much better for everyone concerned if we could just dissolve the marriage and draw up a Family Union contract where all the family can have their say in what they want out of the new relationship.

One of the things that helped me in the early days was the thought, when the children had grown up they would realise that, by walking out, I had not abandoned them but had just done what needed to be done and that no one would leave children they loved and give up a comfortable home, for no reason.

Unfortunately, this has not happened: whether because they have adopted my former husband's attitude towards me or because of the long separation, I don't know. Either way, it still hurts just as much and what really hurts deeply is the fact that in some way it will be affecting them.

I have read and re-read your book and I cannot but admire how you have used your shattering experience to such good effect. It is very comforting to know I am not the only person in this situation. If we can be of any help to others going through this ordeal, I'm sure it would be worthwhile.

This is my story:

I walked out on my husband and two children, daughter 15 and son 10, seventeen years ago. I could no longer love or respect my husband who, over the 20 years of our marriage had physically and mentally abused me. When I realised I had fallen in love with a former colleague of my husband's who had been a close family friend for a number of years, I knew I had to decide whether to go and make a new life for myself or stay and try yet again to save my marriage.

I finally decided to leave. I had very little money and no guarantee my new relationship would work. I knew my children would be better off where they were as I could not be sure of a roof over my head.

My husband would not answer correspondence regarding my seeing the children and I had to wait 5 years for a divorce and 7 years before I got any financial settlement (£8,000 for 20 years of my life). He got the children, the family home and all the contents apart from one or two personal things.

By this time my daughter did not wish to see me, and I saw my son only occasionally. I have not seen my daughter since and have no idea where she is or what she is doing. It is two years since I last saw my son. I still think of them every day.

I am sure there are any number of women out there in a similar situation who have suffered to the point of desperation and suicide, as I did, before walking out on their family, only to be seen as wicked villains, instead of the victims they really are.

I hope this will help other women: it has certainly helped me by writing about it as I am still unable, even after 17 years, to talk to anyone about it. I am pleased to say my relationship did work out and I am now happily married. I did not know I would lose my children but, given the choice, I would do the same again.

The Beginning of The Family Union

"What is the future for the family? In a major speech at the end of July [1998], the Home Secretary joined a growing chorus of politicians, priests and pundits expressing increasing concern for the future of the family and the institution of marriage as the cement which holds society together. Few would challenge the validity of that concern for an institution which is seen by many to be deeply flawed, with an alarming rate of divorce, domestic violence and child abuse...Marriages, at 279,000 a year have reach an all-time low; divorces are now running at 154,000 a year."

Martin Bowley Q.C.,
An End to Sound-Bite Ideas of what makes a Family,
The Independent, 28 August, 1998

In November 1998 the Home Secretary published his Green Paper on the Family encouraging much debate in newspapers, TV and radio for a few months. But did it change anything coming from a government which increasingly denies wanting to "nanny" us but which, in effect, is doing just that?

'People power', magical potent stuff capable of stirring up the Monarchy to bring down flags at half mast, encouraging the Royals to have a 'make-over', is the only force to effectively change grassroots thinking.

One of the causes of deep sometimes permanent suffering among children is the realisation that divorced parents are not going to get together ever again. It is like a joyless well of unhappiness rising up again and again. Being the child of parents who divorced when I was 17 over thirty-five years ago I know this to be true. Each Christmas until my mother died six years ago, I always longed to buy one of those huge padded cards which said "To Mum and Dad".

In Dinosaurs Divorce: A Guide for Changing Families, Laurene Krasny Brown and Marc Brown have illustrated a simple but lively picture book for very young children to guide them through the initial stages of separation and divorce. Young children are recognised to harbour secret dreams:

"Beth often dreams that her parents will marry each other again. But she knows that people who get divorced don't usually get back together again. Even when parents separate children can still love both of them just the same."

Other chapter headings are:

- Feeling upset
- After a divorce
- Living with one parent
- Visiting parents
- Having two homes
- Celebrating holidays and special occasions
- Telling friends
- Meeting parents' new friends
- Living with step-parents
- Stepsisters and stepbrothers

If children could feel their separated parents are still somehow connected through an informal network which we will, for the sake of discussion, call The Family Union, they might be persuaded that divorce is not the end of their family world, that The Family Union might be a workable alternative and might even be an acceptable replacement for the old irreparable marriage or partnership which is about to be dissolved.

It's not going to be perfect, it's obviously second-best and it's going to need working on. Both parents should encourage open discussion with the children. Acknowledge its deficiencies, say it's the best you can do at the moment but ask them to share in the building of this new unit.

All children have intelligence, most have more real perception and insight into your failed marriage than you might have thought possible. The eventual outcome after a lot of work and time, should be such that each child will still feel he/she is still connected to both parents, but most significantly both parents are still connected to each other in the long-term interests of the children.

Although no longer married or living together, you will still be in partnership for them and will need to be in regular contact in the future to talk about their development, their growing needs and their education.

Divorce Source, Inc. which hosts an electronic resource web site at www.divorcesource.com provides a comprehensive range of divorce-related information, primarily for families in the United States. Some issues, however, are pertinent for all divorcing or separating parents wherever they live:

> *"The loss of family structure is very important. Divorce in the family environment requires the family to restructure. Both parents must continue to play an important role in the life of their child.*

> *It is generally a good idea that the parents design a well thought out parenting plan in order to keep some predictability in the family structure. This is good for the sake of the child. Divorce does not have to mean the end of a family.*

> *It is also good for the children to keep close ties with other relatives. Even if you as the parent do not get along with the extended family, children need these people in their lives."*

Both parents may be living far apart, may perhaps have re-married or have new children. The new partner may well bring his/her children from a former relationship into the new family being structured. How confusing and upsetting this must be for children who are virtually coerced into this new family structure and may be encouraged to break ties with the old important one. A formalised Family Union agreement, encompassing all important members of the old extended family with whom the children are linked might, in some families, ease the on-going pain of some children, helping them in their recovery from prolonged agony or grief as they struggle to come to terms with their new role in adjusting to unfamiliar people in intimate surroundings.

A devastating legacy of your splitting-up, unless you and your estranged partner take action from the very beginning, may be lasting damage to your children's social and emotional progress as well as their educational development if their needs are ignored or overlooked in the process of ending your marriage or long-term relationship.

Goodwill, harmony and friendship, even if initially strained or forced, between the parents splitting up can only be positive for the children.

The opposite of these qualities is a deadly and destructive outcome for all concerned for a very long time.

Telling children about Divorce and forming the Family Union

"There are three sides to an argument: his, her's and the truth." Conflict, trying to justify the ending of a marriage with your side of the 'truth' or fault-throwing, is harmful and destructive for everyone. Just as everyone knows some family that has experienced the devastation of a lingering death of a loved one from an incurable disease, so everyone knows someone who has suffered prolonged unhappiness in not coming fully to terms with the effects of a traumatising divorce involving children. This cannot continue from century to century.

Darlene Weburne, a Certified Social Worker in the USA, licensed marriage and family therapist, psychotherapist and interim clinical co-ordinator with Family and Children's Service of Midland, teaches social work at Delta College in Midland, Michigan. Her book, What to Tell the Kids About Your Divorce,

"helps parents move beyond their own anger and hurt to focus on helping their children cope with the divorce. The practical exercises in this book provide parents with the "hands-on" tools they need to help their kids get through all the stages of divorce from the initial separation to later issues of remarriage and step-parenting."

Her guidelines include:

"How, What and When to Tell Your Children About Divorce
Parenting Time (Visitation)
Parenting Rules
Co-parenting
Communicating More Effectively
Understanding and Helping Your Children Express Their Feelings
Age-Specific Reactions to Divorce
Remarriage

Step-parenting
Taking Care of Yourself
Confronting and Coping with Your Feelings"

After the initial shock and heavy sadness felt by the children who may display bad behaviour, withdraw into themselves, throw physical or verbal abuse at one or both parents, a family forum could be held with both partners present to discuss the forming of your unique version of The Family Union.

Both parents must make it abundantly clear to the children from the outset, using appropriate language to suit their ages, that the marriage or relationship is about to be dismantled or undone and nothing will change that one harsh fact. Avoid emotive words like "splitting up", "breaking up" or "divorce" for a while until they have had a chance to get used the idea of initial separation.

The fact that you are both taking the trouble to sit down with them, to explain things simply, clearly and without rancour, will be less far less destructive for your children in the long run than one parent angrily blurting out one version of so-called 'truth' in a scorched earth policy, thereby risking permanently damaging children's vision of the offending parent during childhood or young adulthood.

Children, unless they are babies or toddlers, will remember everything with absolute clarity. However, some solicitors will tell you, even though the children might side in the beginning with the parent who is angry or vindictive, in later years it is highly likely some children will "go over to the other side". With maturity and independence, your children will be the ones ultimately who judge and who may choose in later years to favour the persecuted parent and perhaps reject the persecutor.

It makes sense if you value your children and their future ties with you to do everything you can sensibly and rationally for them.

Regular family forums to discuss the future should not be used as occasions to rake over the past in murderous revenge for past misdeeds.

Go over the past if you must but gently and rationally. If appropriate, discuss some of those differences in the marriage which have bought about its breakdown, which are relevant to the children and which will clarify, by example, why the marriage is being undone.

Again, depending on the ages of the children, the message should be phrased gently: "Mummy/Daddy and I are going to undo our marriage but we are also going into partnership with each other for you." The truth may be hidden in a steel hammer but the blow is softened.

Terry Hillman and Pam Weintraul in their book, Telling Your Kids It's Over, have the following specific advice on how to tell children of all ages that you are parting:

"As soon as you and your spouse have made the decision to separate, it's time to tell your children. Telling your children sooner rather than later will ensure that they don't hear the news from another source or overhear you talking. Deception can promote fantasies about what is really going on, fears of abandonment, wonder about whether they will ever see their departing parent again, and a lack of understanding of the new realities they are about to face. If your children suspect information is being held back, a breach of trust might develop, becoming difficult, if not impossible, to repair."

They suggest that modifications on the following sentences might be useful for a variety of children's ages but emphasise, strongly, that both parents should tell the children *together*:

"**Dad**: As you may know, your Mom and I have not been getting along for a while now. Although we were once happy together, we've grown apart. We tried to work things out and have been seeing a marriage counsellor for quite a while, but we've reached an impasse.
We think we'll be happier if we live separately, so we've decided to get a divorce. You have done nothing to cause us to divorce. It is not your fault. This is between your mother and me.
Mom: I'm sure you know that we both love you very much. Just because your Dad and I don't want to be together anymore doesn't mean that we don't want to be with you. Parents can divorce each other but can't and don't want to divorce their kids. We will be your Mom and Dad forever. We will always be there for you just as before. You will always be taken care of. You will

always have a home. Each of us will be with you, but not at the same time. **Dad**: I have rented an apartment a few blocks away, and I'll be moving there next Saturday. You will be living with your Mom and coming over to live with me every other weekend. We'll also get together once a week for dinner and homework help. We'll be sharing each holiday. I'll call you every night after school, and you can call me anytime. You'll have your own room at my apartment, and you can decorate it any way you want. (If the living arrangement is not yet settled, you can say "The details haven't been worked out yet, but we'll let you know as soon as they are.")

Mom: Your family will always be your family, even though Dad and I aren't going to be in the same house. Your grandparents, aunts, uncles, and cousins will still be your grandparents, aunts, uncles, and cousins.

If you have any questions, you can ask them now, or you can talk to Dad or me later at any time. Remember, we'll always be there for you, and we love you very much."

In Dinosaurs Divorce the chapter Trouble at Home illustrates a picture caption sequence for very young children using the following words:

"Parents don't always get along together. Some parents row. Others don't talk to each other. Joe's mum shouts at him when really she is angry with his dad. When Beth's mother is upset she drinks a lot. She thinks this will make her feel better. Sometimes it is better for parents not to live together any more. They may decide to separate or even divorce."

Children will soon realise, after an association of many ideas which are initially too painful to face up to that their parents have their very best interests at heart, that both making a real effort to undo some of the damage which is going to occur and that both are united on this one issue at least.

The ending of marriage should be programmed like a military exercise for the sake of your children, and be much better planned than your wedding day or the day you moved in together.

Then you exchanged vows with your spouse. Now you must exchange them again but this time with your children present and taking part, conferring with them over terms, conditions, demands, explanations – over and over again until children are satisfied they will not be excluded from both parents' future lives and that both parents will continue to see each other as regularly as possible on a friendly basis.

These vows should have more binding conditions as parents promise to respect each other's differences and be loyal, true and faithful to children, to do their duty with love and conscientiousness.

This can be a pact, a private understanding or a formal contract which can be sealed, signed and ratified with all due solemnity so the children can feel they have taken part in an important and historic family occasion. It could be formalised as a Family Union document which all members sign.

The Family Union might be an informal contract drawn up by the children on the computer or in their own hand rather like an illuminated manuscript, and framed for them to display where they choose, privately on their bedroom wall or publicly in the entrance hall.

It will name all members of the family who would like to be in the Union to ensure links are not severed with the extended family of grandparents, aunts, uncles and cousins as happens in so many cases. Such family members could even sign their own names, perhaps adding a message. My own children, sadly, have lost all contact with my family and some good friends because their father cut them off from anyone who supported me either through the courts or through friendship. If they did get together after a few years, all that comfortable familiarity and special intimacy built up over years of family get-togethers, shared familiar homes, experiences with friends, could never easily be regained.

Involve the children if they are old enough in any financial implications, in decisions about where they would like to live or areas where they might have to live. If the one partner is going to leave the family home without the children, try and look or behave cheerfully and supportively even if you do have a sense of your world coming to an end. It's not, it's just changing.

Encourage the children to look on the changed circumstances as something to look forward to even if it means moving to a smaller home and even if, as is usually the case after divorce, money is going to be short.

- New friends but keeping the old ones.
- Another bedroom, perhaps, in the other parent's home.
- Two sets of pets, toys, books.
- Outings in a different part of town or country.

You may be clutching at straws in an effort to build on the positive. Don't promise the moon if you can't deliver it: just promise you'll always be there for them.

If you want to hold onto your children, let them have the freedom to hold both parents in high esteem. Your children usually have nothing to do with the fundamental reasons why your marriage or relationship has failed.

The Third Party and your Children

Once a few family forums have been held, and the children feel a little easier about the immense changes they are about to experience, the time might be right to introduce the children to the existence of another person about to enter their life (if one exists), having discussed this beforehand, with your, soon to be, ex-partner.

Only you will know how much time you need to discuss such things rationally in front of the children, particularly if the existence of a Third Party is a complete revelation to you, too, and has shattered you to the core.

If you have not initiated the ending of your marriage or relationship, you will feel as if your world has come to an end. The end of marriage, as discussed earlier, is still seen by society as a kind of death. If this is what you feel, you will pass this on to your children, intentionally or not. You and they will in time go through the five stages of grief:

- denial
- anger
- bargaining
- depression
- acceptance

All these are important stages for you, to experience fully and to accept fully. You may find if you skip one stage you may have to go back to the beginning and go through it again. You will discover a kind of inner peace in yourself once you progress to the final stage. I use the word 'progress' because you will have made a long journey. Although you need to reach that goal at your own pace, try to get there as soon as is reasonably possible, accepting or seeking as much help as you can from professional counsellors and support organisations.

This book does not purport to offer you assistance for your grief at the ending of your marriage or long-term relationship. There are many worthy books and people who will guide you through this. My aim is to attempt to make both parents aware of the damage which can be done to children when one or both parents engage in intentionally spiteful, malicious and bitter conflict in post-separation scenarios which alter or irreparably harm children's perceptions of one or both parents.

If there is a third party about to enter the children's lives, this person may or may not be known to them but, in any case, all your lives within the previously safe family environment are about to be uprooted and disrupted as one person's love is withdrawn and given to another, perhaps someone who is a stranger to the children.

There is inevitably going to be an atmosphere of potential destruction for which everyone – children, parents and third party – may be ill-prepared unless the parents and all responsible adults reign in their feelings and take stock of the serious dangers for children:

- Rejection is agonisingly and excruciatingly painful. It will create great disturbance and depression in your life for a while but is something you must deal with quite separately from the children, and with professionals who can help you to work through your feelings.
- Don't involve your children in fuelling feelings of extreme hostility, revenge or anger, however justified, for your spouse/partner and his/her new love.
- Don't involve children in your own feelings of self-pity or victimisation. You don't want to be a victim for ever and self-pity is totally self-destructive if you allow it to flourish.
- Don't involve children in your feelings of failure: the only thing that has

failed is your relationship or marriage, not you, and the reasons for that are only ultimately clear to the two people involved.

- Your children have not failed, you have not failed, your partner has not failed but a relationship between two people has failed and broken down irretrievably.

- Don't involve children in apportioning blame: blaming someone or something may help relieve your feelings of intense anger temporarily but it's a complete waste of energy, hurts children and may potentially damage any future hopes of establishing a new relationship in the very near future within your children's Family Union.

Some children may, understandably in some circumstances, be demanding, unmanageable, and deeply resentful, perhaps even doing their level best to break up new friendships or a strong partnership.

Again, from Dinosaurs Divorcing, the chapter headed Meeting Parents' New Friends has a picture sequence to assist very young children in the process of understanding confusing new situations:

"When mothers and fathers separate they may go out with new friends. It can be fun staying with a baby-sitter. Children sometimes feel jealous and want their parents all to themselves. Luke was always polite to his dad's new friend even though he did not like her at first. After a while she became his friend too."

The aggrieved partner may think that if the children dislike a potential step-parent this might work in his/her favour and may, in some twisted way, bring the partner back. It seldom does. What it will do is make for many unhappy moments with confused children disoriented by new surroundings and strange people. Both parents will have the job of picking up the pieces when hurt, angry or confused children are returned home. The third party is under no obligation to love your children but, if you have your children's best interests at heart, both parents should hope he/she will eventually learn to like your children and will, in time, promote their best interests too.

All responsible adults, parents and extended family must resolve to accept the new situation quickly, and work together for the sake of restoring harmony in children's lives.

Avril's Story

I must congratulate you on all your hard work and I am sure it will be a strong support for parents isolated from their children or who are contemplating leaving a marriage. I could relate to so much in it – so many familiar words spoken by ex-husbands, "You don't know what you've done" and being likened to a prostitute. Being the main disciplinarian and being resented for it. I agree with Irene's comments and felt very sad reading her story, as indeed I did with the others. I found the PAS section particularly interesting and the examples in the Criteria Defining PAS could have been written about my own case history, they were so exact. In fact it was spooky! But it was also comforting as well.

Here is my story.

My life changed when I realised my marriage was not working and I wanted to start afresh. A while before the actual break-up, we talked it over but my ex-husband was against parting, saying it would be too much of an upheaval, we couldn't afford a divorce and it was easier if we just carried on. I was not happy about this but decided not to rock the boat.

Eventually, I met Malcolm and had to make a decision about my future. From the beginning, I was honest about the relationship as I wanted to make it clear this was not a 'fling'. By this time my children were being forced to take sides by my ex-husband who made it clear he was right and I was wrong. Gradually, with the help of his parents, they were brain-washed into believing I was a bad mother whom they hated because I wanted to leave their father.

Thankfully, my youngest child who was four a half at the time did not understand and remained her usual self towards me. I suggested to my ex-husband that he leave and move into his parents' home nearby, or into the house they rented out next door, so I could look after all three children. He stood firm, saying it was his house and he wasn't going. If I wanted to end the marriage I would have to go. He wanted to keep all our children and would fight me all the way.

I endured several weeks of this vendetta then took the only way out. It was New Year's Eve 1994 when I packed Elizabeth's and my belongings into my car and moved into Malcolm's home. If, at any time they had said, "Please don't go" I could never have left. But brain-washing had worked so successfully they couldn't wait for me to go. I was just so thankful Elizabeth had been left untouched, feeling if I stayed any longer she, too, would be taken. I will never forget watching the boys walking along the path with their father to their grandparents' home a few hundred yards away, thinking, from this day on, I shall never be a real mum to them ever again.

I hoped one day my boys would understand I had left their father, not abandoned them. My battle then started. He was prepared to fight me all the way for custody of Elizabeth. My solicitor advised going to conciliation meetings to work out what was best for the children. Court Welfare Officers became involved. The letters from solicitors mounted in costs for me and my new partner as our income, based on my partner's, excluded us – but not my ex-husband – from legal aid.

Trying to build a new relationship, keeping up contact with my reluctant boys, maintaining some form of normality for Elizabeth took its toll. Once you are on this roller-coaster you can't get off. My ex-husband was out to destroy me for breaking up the family. He would succeed through the children.

Another few months elapsed. Just before we were to face the judge, he relented, agreeing it would be better for a daughter to stay with her mother. I was now legally allowed to keep my daughter but he vowed never to speak to me or have anything more to do with me again, a promise he has kept. There were access agreements made which were ignored. It is now over two years since my ex-husband saw our daughter. He has never phoned her or tried to make contact in case I answer the phone. Just a card and present sent at Christmas and birthdays signed, "lots of love, Daddy". But he still holds a place in her heart.

Time moved on. Sometimes the boys were pleasant to me, at other times they were rude, hurtful, their remarks making me feel like the scum of the earth. I still carried on with the phone calls. After the second Christmas passed after I left, my elder son appeared to change his feelings towards me and wanted to start staying over at weekends. I was pleased with his change of heart and encouraged him.

Then, one Saturday, I received a tearful phone call from him saying his father was packing his belongings into a bin liner and throwing him out. Malcolm found him outside his home with his bags on the ground. James had been made to choose between living with my ex-husband and not seeing me or, "If it's so good round there with her, you may as well live there."

At first I was elated having two of my children with me and Elizabeth was happy having James around. He had to settle into a new school and meet new friends which went smoothly. He seemed pleased I was looking after him again and, for a short time, I thought this was going to be as good as it gets. Little by little, things began to go wrong. James and Malcolm did not get on and Malcolm resented having to support both my children, particularly one who didn't get on with him. I have never had any maintenance from my ex-husband as he gave up his job shortly after I left.

I felt torn, reckoning James was reacting in this way because of the situation. He was still nice to me but the atmosphere became unbearable. It was decided James would return to Paul as I couldn't afford to contribute a great deal, financially, earning only a few pounds a week doing cleaning jobs at that time.

The day I helped pack his things was one of the hardest I have had to bear. I felt I had lost my son twice. I miss him terribly. We had been together again for 13 months and the house now seemed empty without him. I agonised over whether there was something I could have done to prevent this latest blow. We continued to speak over the phone but the relationship I had built up crumbled again. There was nothing I could do. He was being made to choose between us and I had lost again.

Several months went by before we could talk again. Visits are still far from relaxed but, sometimes, they are easier than others. But I also feel even further alienated from my boys now as, quite recently, my ex-husband has involved them in a close-knit religious organisation holding radical beliefs. If you are not part of their world, you are an outsider.

I still hope though for a better relationship in the future with my boys. I never start the day without thinking of them, longing to care for them. They are the last thing I think of before I go to sleep.

Badly Broken Down Marriages
and Relationships

"What Is Domestic Violence?"

Domestic violence can take a number of forms, including:

- *physical behaviour such as slapping, punching, pulling hair or shoving.*
- *forced or coerced sexual acts or behaviour such as unwanted fondling or intercourse, or jokes and insults aimed at sexuality.*
- *threats of abuse - threatening to hit, harm or use a weapon on another, or to tell others confidential information.*
- *psychological abuse - attacks on self-esteem, controlling or limiting another's behaviour, repeated insults and interrogation.*

Typically, many kinds of abuse go on at the same time in a household."

Nolo's Everyday Encyclopaedia of Law, California. website: www.nolo.com

If your marriage has broken down badly for reasons to do with sexual and/or physical abuse against you or the children, drugs, alcohol, gambling, and your partner won't acknowledge or discuss these issues, you need to unburden yourself to a professional who will advise you on safety issues. Keep the children safe, above all else, as well as yourself.

Marriage guidance counsellors will see you separately although you may have to wait weeks or months to see some of them. Counsellors found through your doctor, church or Citizens Advice bureaux might see you sooner. See also the list of organisations at the end of this book.

No one can cope with domestic violence alone. You need help if you feel unsafe in your own home. If you have reached this stage then you are living in fear of someone who lives in your home. A leaflet on domestic violence produced by the Lord Chancellor's Department in September 1997 explains how the Family Law Act 1996 strengthens the civil law and can offer you help. It takes courage to ask for help; it takes courage to acknowledge to yourself, let alone to the whole world, that you are a victim. The leaflet offers good advice but taking it is a big step:

"Domestic violence can begin at any stage of a relationship and may continue after the relationship has ended. It can take many forms – not just physical attacks but also bullying, threats, and mental and verbal abuse and humiliation. Women usually experience domestic violence, but this is not always the case; men can be the victims of violence by their women partners. Domestic violence can arise in other family relationships as well. It cuts across all boundaries of social group, class, age, race, disability, sexuality and lifestyle.

Who can apply to the court for an order?

• people who are or have been married to each other
• people who, although not married to each other, are living together or have lived together as husband and wife
• people who live or have lived in the same household (other than as employer and employee, or landlord and tenant or lodger)
• people who have agreed to marry each other (provided that the agreement has not ended more than three years ago)
• the parents of a child, or people with parental responsibility for that child
• where a child is adopted, the natural parents and grandparents of the child, the adoptive parents, and the child

What court orders can be made?

A Non-Molestation Order

This order is about behaviour. It can stop one person pestering, threatening or being violent to another person, or to any child involved.

An Occupation Order

This order is about the home, and can do a number of things. For example, it can:

- order the violent person to leave the home, or a part of it
- order the violent person not to come near the home
- order the violent person to allow the victim of violence to enter and stay in the home, or a part of it
- decide what rights the violent person and the victim of violence have to occupy the home

How do I apply to the court for an order?

You can apply to any magistrates' court or county court with deals with family cases. If you telephone or call in at your local court they will be able to help you or tell you which is the nearest family court. Any member of staff at the enquiry point will be able to help you although they will not be able to give you legal advice. The court will provide you with an application form.

What can I do in an emergency?

- If an order needs to be made urgently, the court has power to do so immediately, before the person against whom the order is being made is told that you have applied.
- The court must consider whether there is a risk of significant harm from that person to you or any child involved if the order is not made immediately.
- If the court makes this type of order, it must allow the person against whom the order has been made an opportunity to put their side of the case. This will happen at a further hearing to which everyone involved can come and give evidence.

Can I get Legal Aid to apply?

Yes, if you can show that your savings and your income are within the current financial limits."

Although I have known a few violent women, and in one case a women who attacked her husband on several occasions with a knife, violence against women by men is more common. It is one reason why some marriages or relationships break down very badly and can lead to women leaving home without warning very suddenly without their children. They are powerless to do anything, having been hammered down emotionally and physically over a number of years, with the loss of self-confidence as well as self-respect. A web site in Australia, the Women's Resource Information and Support Centre offer the following information on domestic violence:

- "Domestic Violence is the most common form of assault in Australia
- Each year in Victoria between 30 and 40 women and children are killed by their husbands, boyfriends, ex-partners, fathers and sons.
- One in seven married women will be subjected to domestic violence.
- Where women kill their partners, it is well documented that it is likely to have been as a result of a long history of being victimised by them.
- 97% of domestic violence offenders are male.
- Domestic violence includes physical abuse, mental torture, emotional abuse, sexual abuse, social deprivation, public humiliation, verbal assaults and financial control.
- Alongside domestic violence, sexual assault is probably the most under reported crime of the century.
- The myths that surround domestic violence (alcohol or stress-related, men do it; that women ask for it, that it should be kept in the family) are lies that keep women and children from telling.
- Realising that you are not to blame is one of the first steps to healing."

The Women's Resource Information and Support Centre offer some answers to the myths and realities of domestic violence whereby myths "allow abusers to shift the responsibility for their violence to the victim, or someone/thing else."

MYTH: If a woman doesn't like it she can leave.
- "It's your own fault you're in this situation".
- "No-one is keeping you there, you must be happy to put up with it".

REALITY: Women cannot always leave, some reasons include fear, lack of money, lack of information, because of the children, thinking he will change. NB The ramifications can be more serious if she does leave.

MYTH: Alcohol consumption is the most common cause of domestic violence.
- "I didn't know I was doing it"
- "I won't drink any more"

REALITY : Alcohol is not the reason for violence, it is used as an excuse or gives some men the courage to abuse.

MYTH: Women only get beaten when they 'ask' for it.
- "You should learn to keep your mouth shut"
- "I warned you"

REALITY : No-one deserves or asks to be hurt.

MYTH: Violence happens mostly in poor peoples homes.
- "They are poor and uneducated, they don't understand what they are doing"

REALITY: Violence occurs in all economic groups.

MYTH: Violent men come from violent homes.
- "It wasn't his fault, he had a really awful upbringing"

REALITY : Not all abusers come from violent homes.

MYTH: You only hurt those whom you love.
- "He's really jealous, that's why he lashes out"

REALITY : No-one has the right to hurt you.

MYTH: Domestic violence isn't a big problem.
- "I don't know anyone in that situation"
- "It doesn't happen around here"

REALITY : Domestic violence is a big problem, it is just hidden."

If you and the children have become victims of violence you need to seek urgent help and advice from authorities such as the police or social workers. There are other non-authority organizations which can help (see at the back of this book) or go to your local Citizens Advice Bureau as soon as possible who will advise on where you can seek help or where perhaps you and the children can shelter in a temporary refuge. Don't wait and 'hope it will get better'.

If your marriage or relationship has broken down very badly for reasons other than violence, again, you need to seek advice. Sometimes it is not easy to get help or advice quickly and you may have to wait. You've been patient for a long while so try and keep busy while you're waiting for the longed-for appointment.

In my own case, my former husband refused on many, many occasions to discuss conflicting issues with me or to visit a counsellor with me in the early years of our marriage. At that time I was seriously intent on trying to put things right, in trying to make us both confront issues which we could not do together without it developing into a fault-finding heated row in which both slung accusations at each other, raking up the past with old grievances which neither of us would put to rest. After I left him, he made an appointment to see one and begged me to go with him. I refused. It was by then far too late.

On reflection, I should have gone because most counsellors are trained to advise if they feel the marriage has broken down irretrievably and is indeed at an end. Sometimes that message is more easily accepted from a third-party professional.

Marital counselling is also known as couples counselling and Liz Hodgkinson in her book, Counselling, believes that in order for such counselling to work, both partners "have to agree that they have problems which they cannot sort out for themselves and for which they feel they need some expert help".

If couples are having regular disagreements on many issues and can't agree on mundane things let alone important issues in their daily lives, it is usually impossible to find both of them agreeing to see a couples or marital counsellor. This is usually the biggest problem, according to Liz Hodgkinson:

"Frequently, if one partner mentions the possibility of counselling, the other will resist the idea strongly and may actively sabotage it. This is probably a reflection of the problems in the relationship where the individuals no longer see eye to eye. What may have seemed endearing at one time has become profoundly irritating. In growing up, partners often grow apart and usually one recognises this while the other does not. But if one partner won't agree to counselling, it does not mean that the other cannot go to seek help alone – indeed, this is very common."

Liz Hodgkinson cautions against people believing that counselling is going to solve all ills or even some of the main reasons for wanting to have marital counselling:

"...One of the main tasks of the counsellor is to enable partners to appreciate that it is not possible ever to change the behaviour of another person. Unless that person sincerely wants to change and is committed to doing so, then there is no room for manoeuvre. Any suggestion that the person may change is usually met with enormous resistance. 'Why should I change?' the partner asks. 'You are the one who needs to change your attitudes.' Until deadlocks like this can be broken, little can be achieved.

...Couples counselling attempts to break down hostilities, to provide an environment where each partner can talk freely, with the counsellor acting as referee. The counsellor should not take sides but should be able to assess the situation for what it is and see the hidden agenda behind the apparent one.

Nikki, who with her now ex-husband Gerald went for couples counselling when their marriage hit severe problems said: 'Things got so bad that in the end the only way we could communicate with each other was through the counsellor. Although the marriage broke up in the end, it was achieved with far less rancour than would have happened without counselling."

If you are deeply unhappy and really cannot wait any longer, try to find a counsellor or legal aid solicitor who will see you separately, if only to discuss the legal and financial issues involved in dismantling a marriage and the complex issues involved if there are children. He may refer you to other specialists. If so, go and see them immediately. This will keep you busy and give you some sort of a framework or structure to your daily life.

The library can also be a great source of help with reference works on divorce as well as books by people who have experienced it.

Your doctor if he's anything like mine may be helpful too and offer other support which you may have overlooked in your misery. One can never have too much advice when your own and your children's lives are at stake. You may think being over-loaded with advice and help will only confuse you but you will sift through it all at your leisure and eventually come up with the answers which are right for you.

Some professional advice may help you to concentrate on the practical issues:

- when to leave
- where to live – temporarily
- how to pay for it

Leave aside your deep unhappiness which now seems to well up daily, and put it into a mental compartment while you carry on with day-to-day life. When you are heavily involved in weighing up the emotional costs for yourself and your children, set and meet minor deadlines to keep sane and concentrate on practical and financial issues.

This may even help you decide to stay and see things through for a while longer. If not, it may help you in coming to terms with the ending of your marriage.

STAYING FOR THE MOMENT

The thought of leaving has probably occurred to you maybe just once or perhaps a hundred times but you have pushed it again and again from your mind as an impossible solution for the present.

So you stay but perhaps you have a secret dream or even a loosely formed plan which you bring to the front of your mind, most frequently when you are on autopilot: travelling to work, cutting the grass, loading the washing machine, sitting in front of the computer, walking the children to school, washing the kitchen floor, watching TV with the family.

You think you should stay for now but have a sketchy plan which keeps you going and allows you temporary satisfaction.

You will wait

- until the children are older because they need both a father and a mother at home.

- until the children start school/finish their GCSEs/A-levels/ leave school.
- until they start university/leave university so their studying, concentration, equilibrium is not upset
- until her/his mother or father recovers from a serious illness/celebrates an anniversary/comes out of hospital/comes back from holiday
- until they get settled in the new home/surroundings/residential care

so no one is upset by your action.

You imagine many people may be disappointed or feel betrayed, if you leave. Many people at work, at home, in your social life may be shocked, perhaps disappointed.

It suddenly occurs to you these people have opinions you perhaps value or respect. The opinions of people in your family network may also matter. They may not only value you as well but may expect you to provide them with unquestioning support across a wide network of services.

This may have to come to an end if you leave. And what about the dismantling of the marriage and home organisation you have built up over a decade or two or three? What about the removal not only of personal possessions but the decisions needed on who really owns what?

And what if your partner is violent or capable of violence, if the arguments you've had are anything to go by? How should you go? In cold blood, having planned every detail?

Or as I did, in the heat of yet another argument late one night, walking out on everything, leaving him the luxury later of flinging out not only all my most precious keep-sakes, trinkets, treasured papers, scraps of my girlhood, womanhood and motherhood, but also the leisure to reinvent my past as a mother so the children could "divorce" me at the same time as he did.

The time somehow never seems right and you push it once again to the back of your mind until, in a heated moment of high family drama, you walk out.

Don't. Don't, under any circumstances, just walk out without having a plan and without having prepared yourself, your partner but, most importantly, your children. You risk losing everything from your children to the roof over your head and you risk causing immense pain and ongoing suffering to your children.

Another web site on the Internet supporting divorced parents and families, www.SmartDivorce.com have printed a letter from a teenager which could be a general plea from all children to parents who are about to split up:

> *"Hello everyone,*
>
> *I'm 14 and my parents have been separated since I was 2, divorced when I was 12.*
>
> *I just wanted to offer you all one small piece of advice. After a divorce make sure you stay in touch with your kids. It is the hardest thing in the world for a child to not know where their mother or father is and not know for sure that they love them.*
>
> *My father made the mistake of losing touch without ever explaining why to me, my brother, and my sister. My brother and sister now hate him and will have nothing to do with him. I have managed to get in touch with him and have seen him twice in the past three years, but he still will not call my house. If I want to talk to him I need to call him.*
>
> *Never let this happen between you and your kids. It causes so much unnecessary pain for both sides involved.*
>
> *Also, if you're planning on getting a divorce don't just leave in the middle of the night thinking no one is watching. I saw my father preparing to leave and, even though I was young at the time, I can remember it like it was yesterday. My father doesn't know that I saw him. This memory has haunted me for so long. If my dad had just told me he was leaving it would have made it easier on me and my siblings.*
>
> *Please just think about what I have said.*
>
> *Jill"*

If you have a plan, work on it, research it, seek professional opinions from Citizens' Advice to legal aid solicitors. Plan the end of your marriage with as much care as you planned the beginning of it but use professionals, not friends and family.

Thinking about the right time to leave is sometimes the only thing keeping you going. Your mind is active with the plan and it gives you a framework in which to keep up the pretence of maintaining the outward signs of a working marriage. Your plan becomes your friend because you have no one else to tell. One part of you longs to tell the world, the other part feels it is a selfish thing to do.

If you do in a weak moment mention it to a friend, the reaction may not be what you expect. You may hope for reassurance what you want to do is right. You may be seeking permission that what you want to do is the proper thing to do. If this is not given, you may feel hurt and angry with – or betrayed by – that friend and condemn yourself for having weakened. Now that friend has your secret knowledge and may share it with someone else.

You may be embarrassed if that friend continues to be in your circle of friends, comes into contact with you and your spouse or partner at parties, the school gate, the supermarket or social functions. How should you react now with that friend? It gives you further anxiety at a time when your anxiety should be lessened, not heightened.

If the friend is not judgmental but wants to sit on the fence, that might not be the reaction you wanted either. If the friend is deeply sympathetic, you might feel guilty she/he now has to carry some share of your burden and that is not what friends are for. So there's another layer of guilt to add to the pile you already carry.

Whatever your age and whether you are a man or a woman, you have a pride in keeping up a brave front, a mask to keep up the facade of a happy marriage or a good family life, in maintaining a stoicism because this seems to be instinctive. No one likes to fail.

If you are a mother, you know that society still views the wife, more so than the husband, as the mainstay of a marriage or as the one who keeps the home fires burning. If the marriage is failing, then you shoulder much of the blame, believing it must somehow be your fault.

A father may, be the financial mainstay of the family but a woman is held responsible for providing the outward signs of a successful marriage and a fully functioning family unit which reaches out to support the extended family too.

For the Sake of the Children

So you stay because it's easier to bear the brunt of home, social and work burdens rather than the brunt of, what you imagine will be, people's judgement, whether at home or at work. But the main reason you stay, is for the sake of your children.

You've decided to stay because you care deeply about the effect a walking-out, separation or divorce might have on them. You might even be prepared to give your partner yet another chance. You may decide to attend couples counselling together.

As a parent you cannot imagine facing the social stigma of walking out of your home, of leaving your children, of putting yourself first. No one will know about the inner turmoil, the people you've sought advice from and the sleepless nights when you tossed and turned for weeks or months while considering all the alternatives. The reasons you've decided to stay are many and various but the important thing is you've decided, for now.

Having decided to stay in an unhappy marriage, you must immediately develop a strategy of caring for yourself. Acknowledge the situation to yourself, even if you can't confide in friends, that you know you have a deeply unhappy relationship with your partner but you have decided to stay and stick it out until – whatever reasons you have decided upon.

Different methods work for different people and you must allow time to experiment, finding something which works for you.

If it helps to write down things, make sure you have a secure place, even outside the home, to hide a notebook listing books, organisations, self-help groups or therapists that may help you to take care of yourself. No one else is going to do it and no one else is going to care as much for you as you do for yourself. You have your own best interests at heart. You are your own best friend.

If you've decided to stay, in spite of your partner's behaviour, make sure you and the children are safe and not in any danger from the excessive forces of his/her behaviour in any manner whatsoever. Consider seeing a solicitor if you think you are only going to stay temporarily for whatever reason, so a draft separation or divorce proceedings can be drawn up and put "on hold" pending the outcome of your partner's resumption of behaviour which has endangered you or the children.

Arrange to have important papers, or assemble treasured possessions, in one place so these can be scooped up in a moment. You could then rest easy, relatively, with the knowledge you have arranged everything but nothing need be actioned unless the situation changes dramatically. When, or if, a potentially dangerous situation does occur, you need only to alert your solicitor by telephone if necessary, and action can be immediate.

But it is foolish to put yourself and your children in danger by staying in a situation which may result in physical or psychological harm in the short or long term.

Sarah's Story

Thank you for your manuscript. I shed a lot of tears. There are so many similarities to what I went through when I left. There never is an easy way to leave but, had I known I would lose my children, I would have stayed and continued to suffer. I'm suffering now but it is a different kind of pain. I found your story heart-breaking. It left me feeling emotionally drained but also amazed at how strong and positive you are.

Five years have passed since I left my then 6 year old daughter and 15 year old son and still have not come to terms with it. I really don't like myself at all and not a night goes by when I don't cry.

I really wanted to tell you my story but it is so painful for me to think about that awful day when I took her to school then walked out of her life. I see my daughter on Saturday for a few hours and am so glad if she is loving towards me. I think I lost the right to expect anything from her.

My son is 21 now and is very unforgiving. How can I expect anything else. I can't even forgive myself. I know I will never be truly happy. Separation from my children cannot break the bond and I yearn to mother my children, specially my daughter. I have met a wonderful man who makes my life worth living.

Mothers in our situation deserve all the happiness we get because the price we pay for it is almost too much to bear. I was never selfish in ending my marriage. It took 22 agonising years and a lot of soul searching. My three eldest daughters had left home and had grown up knowing how unhappy I was. They gave me a lot of support when I left.

I know I was leaving an unhappy marriage but my two children must have felt so abandoned. I had been with my husband since I was 16 after coming out of a children's home, having been abandoned by my own mother. So I know what my children went through that day. I was slowly dying in my marriage and to survive I had to sacrifice my children's security and happiness. Nothing there to be proud of. There is a price to pay for everything and I'm paying the price every day.

Thank you again for the privilege of reading your book. Even though it can't ease my pain, it has made me realise that I am not a wicked person and, maybe one day, please God, I will forgive myself and my heartache will ease a little.

Parental Alienation Syndrome

After completing the first draft of this book, I learned, quite by chance, about The Parental Alienation Syndrome first identified by Dr. Richard Gardner M.D. in 1985. Dr. Gardner is a practising child psychiatrist and adult psychoanalyst in the United States who has lectured widely around the world.

Certified in psychiatry, child psychiatry by the American Board of Psychiatry and neurology, Dr. Gardner is a Life Fellow of the American Psychiatric Association, a Fellow of the American Academy of Child and Adolescent Psychiatry and the American Academy of Psychoanalysis. He is currently Clinical professor of Child Psychiatry at the College of Physicians and Surgeons, Columbia University, USA. He has also served as Visiting Professor of Child Psychiatry at the University of Louvain in Belgium and the University of St. Petersburg in Russia. His book The Boys and Girls Book about Divorce (1970) has become standard reading for children of divorce in the USA. This large extract on PAS was taken in August 1999 from his pages on the Internet:

"Since the 1970s, we have witnessed a burgeoning of child-custody disputes unparalleled in history. This increase has primarily been the result of two recent developments in the realm of child-custody litigation, namely, the replacement of the tender-years presumption with the best-interests-of-the-child presumption and the increasing popularity of the joint-custodial concept. The assumption was made that mothers, by virtue of the fact that they are female, are intrinsically superior to men as child rearers. Accordingly, the father had to provide to the court compelling evidence of serious maternal deficiencies before the court would even consider assigning primary custodial status to the father. Under its replacement, the best-interests-of-the-child presumption, the courts were instructed to ignore gender in custodial considerations and evaluate only parenting capacity, especially factors that related to the best interests of the child. This change resulted in a burgeoning of custody litigation as fathers now found themselves with a greater opportunity to gain primary custodial status. Soon thereafter the joint-custodial concept came into vogue, eroding even further the time that custodial mothers were given with their children. Again, this change also brought about an increase and intensification of child-custody litigation.

In association with this burgeoning of child-custody litigation, we have witnessed a dramatic increase in the frequency of a disorder rarely seen previously, a disorder that I refer to as the parental alienation syndrome (PAS). In this disorder we see not only programming ("brainwashing") of the child by one parent to denigrate the other parent, but self-created contributions by the child in support of the alienating parent's campaign of denigration against the alienated parent. Because of the child's contribution I did not consider the terms brainwashing, programming, or other equivalent words to be applicable. Accordingly, in 1985, I introduced the term parental alienation syndrome to cover the combination of these two contributing factors. In accordance with this use of the term I suggest this definition of the parental alienation syndrome:

The parental alienation syndrome (PAS) is a disorder that arises primarily in the context of child-custody disputes. Its primary manifestation is the child's campaign of denigration against a parent, a campaign that has no justification. It results from the combination of a programming (brainwashing) parent's indoctrinations and the child's own contributions to the vilification of the target parent. When true parental abuse and/or neglect is present the child's animosity may be justified, and so the parental alienation syndrome explanation for the child's hostility is not applicable.

THE PARENTAL ALIENATION SYNDROME IS NOT THE SAME AS PROGRAMMING BRAINWASHING

It has come as a surprise to me from reports in both the legal and mental health literature that the definition of the PAS is often misinterpreted. Specifically, there are many who use the term as synonymous with parental brainwashing or programming. No reference is made to the child's own contributions to the victimisation of the targeted parent. Those who do this have missed an extremely important point regarding the etiology, manifestations, and even the treatment of the PAS. The term PAS refers only to the situation in which the parental programming is combined with the child's own scenarios of disparagement of the vilified parent. Were we to be dealing here simply with parental indoctrination, I would have simply retained and utilised the terms brainwashing and/or programming. Because the campaign of denigration involves the aforementioned combination, I decided a new term was warranted, a term that would encompass both contributory factors. Furthermore, it was the child's contribution that led me to my concept of the etiology and pathogenesis of this disorder. The understanding of the child's contribution is of importance in implementing the therapeutic guidelines described in this book.

THE RELATIONSHIP BETWEEN THE PARENTAL ALIENATION SYNDROME AND BONA FIDE ABUSE AND/OR NEGLECT

Unfortunately, the term parental alienation syndrome is often used to refer to the animosity that a child may harbour against a parent who has actually abused the child, especially over an extended period. The term has been used to apply to the major categories of parental abuse: physical, sexual, and emotional. Such application indicates a misunderstanding of the PAS. The term PAS is applicable only when the target parent has not exhibited anything close to the degree of alienating behaviour that might warrant the campaign of vilification exhibited by the child. Rather, in typical cases the victimised parent would be considered by most examiners to have provided normal, loving parenting or, at worst, exhibited minimal impairments in parental capacity. It is the exaggeration of minor weaknesses and deficiencies that is the hallmark of the PAS. When bona fide abuse does exist, then the child's responding alienation is warranted and the PAS diagnosis is not applicable.

Programming parents who are accused of inducing a PAS in their children will sometimes claim that the children's campaign of denigration is warranted because of bona fide abuse and/or neglect perpetrated by the denigrated parent. Such indoctrinating parents may claim that the counter-accusation by the target parent of PAS induction by the programming parent is merely a "cover up," a diversionary manoeuvre, and indicates attempts by the vilified parent to throw a smoke screen over the abuses and/or neglect that have justified the children's acrimony. There are some genuinely abusing and/or neglectful parents who will indeed deny their abuses and rationalise the children's animosity as simply programming by the other

:ent. This does not preclude the existence of truly innocent parents who e indeed being victimised by an unjustifiable PAS campaign of denigration. When such cross-accusations occur – namely, bona fide abuse and/or neglect versus a true PAS – it behoves the examiner to conduct a detailed inquiry in order to ascertain the category in which the children's accusations lie, i.e., true PAS or true abuse and/or neglect. In some situations, this differentiation may not be easy, especially when there has been some abuse and/or neglect and the PAS has been superimposed upon it, resulting thereby in much more deprecation than would be justified in this situation. It is for this reason that detailed inquiry is often crucial if one is to make a proper diagnosis. Joint interviews, with all parties in all possible combinations, will generally help uncover "The Truth" in such situations.

THE PARENTAL ALIENATION SYNDROME AS A FORM OF CHILD ABUSE

It is important for examiners to appreciate that a parent who inculcates a PAS in a child is indeed perpetrating a form of emotional abuse in that such programming may not only produce lifelong alienation from a loving parent, but lifelong psychiatric disturbance in the child. A parent who systematically programs a child into a state of ongoing denigration and rejection of a loving and devoted parent is exhibiting complete disregard of the alienated parent's role in the child's upbringing. Such an alienating parent is bringing about a disruption of a psychological bond that could, in the vast majority of cases, prove of great value to the child–the separated and divorced status of the parents notwithstanding. Such alienating parents exhibit a serious parenting deficit, a deficit that should be given serious consideration by courts when deciding primary custodial status. Physical and/or sexual abuse of a child would quickly be viewed by the court as a reason for assigning primary custody to the non-abusing parent. Emotional abuse is much more difficult to assess objectively, especially because many forms of emotional abuse are subtle and difficult to verify in a court of law. The PAS, however, is most often readily identified, and courts would do well to consider its presence a manifestation of emotional abuse by the programming parent.

Accordingly, courts do well to consider the PAS programming parent to be exhibiting a serious parental deficit when weighing the pros and cons of custodial transfer. I am not suggesting that a PAS-inducing parent should automatically be deprived of primary custody, only that such induction should be considered a serious deficit in parenting capacity–a form of emotional abuse–and that it be given serious consideration when weighing the custody decision. In this book, I provide specific guidelines regarding the situations when such transfer is not only desirable, but even crucial, if the children are to be protected from lifelong alienation from the targeted parent."

It was a revelation to me that part of the circumstances arising between my children and me, one which I thought was relevant only to my own particular situation, had been documented by Dr. Gardner in the United States 14 years ago.

PAS-inducing parents

For more than two decades Dr. Gardner has not only written and lectured widely on PAS and his theories surrounding its effects on children and adults but has also closely observed many clinical examples since the early 1980s.

Among child psychiatrists he is recognised as one of the leading innovators in the field and as a clinical psychiatrist has often been called upon to be an expert independent witness. He has evaluated many children believed to be suffering from PAS and has conducted in-depth studies of the personality traits of typical PAS-inducing parents.

I am not qualified to comment on the validity of Dr. Gardner's theory on the behaviour, predisposition or psychological health patterns of PAS-inducing parents. My book merely touches on the vast subject of PAS but for those parents and professionals interested in further research, I refer you to his comprehensive book on the subject, **The Parental Alienation Syndrome** (2nd ed.), and particularly the chapter Hysteria, Paranoia and Psychopathy from which I have chosen three quotes:

"An in-depth understanding of hysteria, paranoia, and psychopathy will place the reader in a better position to appreciate the subtleties of the parental alienation syndrome."

"The individual reacts in an exaggerated fashion to events and situations that others would either not respond to at all or respond to with only

minimal emotional reaction. In hysteria individuals react with excessive tension, anxiety, agitation, and even acting out. Alienating parents typically overreact in situations that others would not consider justifiable causes of concern. And this is especially the case with regard to the children's complaints about the targeted parent."

"Paranoids often have a family history of significant psychiatric disturbance, whether or not hospitalisation was warranted for these family members. Some readers may consider there to be an inconsistency between my early statement that paranoia is ubiquitous and my statement here that paranoids often have a family history of significant psychiatric disorder. I do not consider there to be an inconsistency here because family dysfunction is also widespread. Accordingly, hospitalised paranoids, as well as those 'on the outside', are likely to come from families in which there has been significant psychiatric dysfunction."

PAS-ABUSED CHILDREN

In a chapter entitled Clinical Manifestations in the Child, Dr. Gardner gives many examples of children obsessed with "hatred" of a parent in which

"these children speak of the alienated parent with every vilification and profanity in their vocabulary – without embarrassment or guilt."

Stressing many times in his book that true PAS has <u>two</u> vital components brought into it by <u>two</u> protagonists to achieve its objective, Dr. Gardner wants readers to understand clearly that it is these two components which provide true PAS:

"the alienating parent's indoctrinations

and

the child's contributions.

It is this combination that warrants the PAS diagnosis."

In other words, PAS has to have the intervention of a child. In illustrating how PAS children manifest their symptoms by giving actual clinical examples, Dr. Gardner warns that:

"some of these may appear unlikely, and even outlandish, to some readers. However, I can assure the reader that every one of these examples, as preposterous as many of them appear to be, are valid ones, their absurdity notwithstanding. In fact, it was the ludicrousness of many of these that led me to my understanding of the basic underlying psychodynamic factors operative in the PAS."

One of the earliest children Dr. Gardner evaluated in a child-custody dispute was Billy, a seven-year-old boy. Billy's memorable exchange of dialogue with him in a clinical session took place whilst Billy's mother was present. (The previous week Billy had had to miss an appointment because of the death of his paternal grandfather.)

"Gardner: I'm very sorry to hear that your grandfather died.
Billy: You know, he just didn't die. My father murdered him.
Gardner (incredulously):Your father murdered your grandfather, his own father?
Billy: Yes. I know he did it.
Gardner: I thought your grandfather was in the hospital? I understand that he was about 85 years old and that he was dying of old-age disease.
Billy: Yeah, that what my father says.
Gardner: What do you say?
Billy: I say my father murdered him in the hospital.
Gardner: How did he do that?
Billy: He sneaked into the hospital, at night, and did it while no one was looking. He did it while the nurses and the doctors were asleep.
Gardner: How do you know that?
Billy: I just know it!
Gardner: Did anyone tell you any such thing?
Billy: No, but I just know it.
Gardner (now turning to the mother, who is witness to this conversation): What do you think about what Billy just said?
Mother: Well, I don't really think that my husband did it, but I wouldn't put it past that son-of-a-bitch!*

Dr. Gardner gives other clinical examples of PAS children and PAS-inducing parents during therapy sessions he has personally conducted over the years, further examples of the two-factor combination which gives rise to the syndrome:

> "One child told me that in school assignments, when he has to write the word dad, he writes DOG instead. Another told me, 'I've memorised my lawyer's telephone number just in case I have to call him when I'm at my father's house.' When I asked him if there ever had been a situation in which he felt he needed to call his lawyer, he replied in the negative. However, he stated that it was good to have that number in his pocket. He claimed that his mother gave him a card with the lawyer's number on it, 'just in case'. He further informed me that his mother reminded him to take that card before each visit. We see here an excellent example of the mother's programming and the child's delusion that he needed such protection."

The alienated parent, who almost certainly enjoyed a good, normal and loving relationship with his child up to the time of separation or divorce, is suddenly reinvented, almost overnight, into an object of venomous hatred and now becomes an object of unremitting scornful abuse, about which PAS children feel absolutely no guilt. Indeed, any anguish displayed by the hurt parent seems to give further gratification to the child and almost becomes an orgiastic 'feast' to be enjoyed at his expense:

> "One child, during a two-hour court-ordered visitation, was brought to a restaurant by his father. As soon as the child got into the car he said, 'The only reason I'm here is because the judge said I have to come.'
>
> The father invited him to select a restaurant, and he responded, 'Choose any shit-hole place you'd like to eat in. I don't give a shit.'
>
> He said absolutely nothing to his father during the ride to the restaurant and, when there, poked his nose in the menu for about 10 minutes without saying a word to his father. He then got up and said, 'I've got to call my mother. She told me to call her to make sure that I'm all right.' When the father asked him, politely, to make it quick, he responded, 'I'll speak to her as long as I want, and what I'll be saying to her is none of your fucking business.'

Twice during the meal he called his mother, each call lasting between 10 and 15 minutes. Not surprisingly, he refused to eat the elaborate and expensive meal that he ordered, claiming, 'This food tastes like shit; why don't you bring it home in a doggie bag and give it to your girlfriend?'"

And in other example:

"Two boys, ages 13 and 15, went to a restaurant with their father. They literally threw their food in his face, and one turned over a bowl of soup on his head. Not surprisingly, the manager asked them to leave the restaurant immediately. As they walked out they mocked him loudly with vile profanities, loud enough for all around to hear. There was absolutely no appreciation for the father's mortification. Probably the only person on earth who would put up with such sadistic treatment is a loving parent, and it is testament to this man's deep affection for his sons that he still 'hung in there' after his humiliation in the restaurant which, not surprisingly, was not an isolated example of their cruelty."

And:

"In one family session with a PAS family, the father was crying bitterly and begging the children to be sympathetic to him. Soon after he began crying, the older boy began laughing at him, and his younger sister immediately followed suit. The older one said, 'There's nothing I like more than to see you cry.' The mother sat by and said absolutely nothing. When I asked her what thoughts she had about what had just gone on, she replied, 'Doctor, I've said it many times. I want to be left out of it. It's between them and him.'"

There is no space in **Lost Children** for any more examples such as these and, indeed, Dr. Gardner believes he could fill a book containing only examples of similar case studies. Parents who are in the early stages of separation or divorce proceedings, following a high-conflict situation, may now begin to recognise the pattern of PAS, to identify a typical PAS-inducing parent, a typical PAS abused child and be ready to take preventative action to avoid this in their own situation.

Those tragic parents who have already lost children may have recognised these typical behaviour trends in their own children or ex-partners. More importantly, some may begin to ask what, if anything, can be done to reverse children's attitude or behaviour which seems cruel, callous and out-of-character. Is it irreversible? Could therapy help? Who will enforce it? Will children attend? What can you do if they won't attend?

Unfortunately, the prognosis for change or the outlook for positive reversal therapy remains bleak and it would be unkind to put hope for improvement into the minds or hearts of those parents who have already lost children.

Dr. Gardner believes

"It is still too early to know exactly what happens to children who have been subjected to years of such alienation. As mentioned, the psychological bond can withstand just so much attenuation before it snaps completely and irrevocably. It is too early for follow-up studies. However, studies are starting to be conducted. Johnston (1993) followed PAS children into mid-adolescence and found most still remained withdrawn and maintained their stance of rejection and denigration of the targeted parent.

Yet all these terrible consequences are preventable in most cases. Not only can the development of the disorder be prevented, but its perpetuation arrested when it does arise. It is my hope that this book [The Parental Alienation Syndrome] will play a role in bringing this rectifiable situation to the attention of those professionals, both in the legal and mental health realms, who are in a position to bring about the prevention and eradication of this widespread psychiatric disturbance."

Although it would be very unwise to hold out hope for full or partial reconciliation or even an improvement in children's personal attitudes, parents should have small, realistic, achievable aims for their own sanity and perhaps think about working towards highlighting their own tragic cases. Getting together with similar parents, forming pressure groups and campaigning for change using whatever means and media are available is one way of directing energies into positive channels. There is much work to be done.

Persuading legal and mental health professions to take note of injustice is an uphill task for those parents already severely disillusioned by these institutions, professions which seemingly 'allow' emotional abuse of children to continue by closing their eyes to it. This cannot be regarded as acting 'in the best interests of the children'. Dr. Gardner holds out little hope at present of an enlightened or intelligent judicial system being prepared to act decisively:

"...PAS-indoctrinating parents recognise that time is on their side. They know that the court's predictable delay is likely to result in an ever-deepening entrenchment of the children's campaign of denigration, lessening thereby the likelihood of his reversibility. With rare exception, one can always count on court delays...By the time the court has gotten around to hearing the case, the children's alienation may be irreversible and the court remains impotent."

REVENGE

"Syndromes are part of everyday diagnosis. The number described seems to increase weekly. Until now, few were known or documented accurately. Just what are these conditions so labelled?

The Oxford English Dictionary defines a 'syndrome' as a 'concurrence of several symptoms in a disease; a set of such concurrent symptoms'. Put in simpler terms, a 'syndrome' can be described as a specific collection of signs and symptoms which when put together form a recognisable pattern which can be seen to be repeated in another individual.

There are now over 2000 of these syndromes recorded. Some are incredibly rare, others uncommon, whilst others are relatively frequently seen in comparison."

Patricia Gilbert,
The A-Z Reference Book of Syndromes and Inherited Disorders
Visiting Senior Lecturer, Warwick University, UK

The above passage referring to chronic medical syndromes is taken from a book mostly concerned with genetically inherited conditions. However, it seems since I 'discovered' PAS and the work of Dr. Richard Gardner that many other divorce-related syndromes or patterns of revenge have been identified or labelled by clinical psychologists in the United States following research into various forms of post-divorce and post-separation responses to splitting-up by one or both parents.

Most of the syndromes which are described in this chapter follow a pattern in that one parent is chronically or morbidly preoccupied with reprisals, retaliation and vengeance to get back at his/her partner for destroying a marriage or relationship. Manipulation of children's previous affection for the target parent, who has supposedly violated the family unit by leaving it, is the final objective of the 'wounded' parent in order to alter the 'offending' parent's position with the children. In nearly all cases, children are used as a facilitating tool to assist the aggrieved parent in the total destruction or annihilation of the children's love or regard for the other parent.

Success and satisfaction is measured by one parent having sole "ownership" of the children's minds and physical presence as well as achieving total defeat of the love, affection or regard in which children previously held the alienated parent.

If the target parent continues to have "part-ownership" of the children through a court ruling, on-going acrimony directed through and at the children makes it almost impossible for them to settle comfortably into a new pattern of family life in two homes without a number of grievous anxieties arising from persistent animosity.

In The Spectrum of Parental Alienation Syndrome (Part 1), Deirdre Conway Rand identifies several of these syndromes, particularly in high conflict divorces.

Medea Syndrome

"The need for revenge is taken to an extreme in Medea Syndrome (4,5). 'Modern Medeas do not want to kill their children but they do want revenge on their former wives or husbands – and they exact it by destroying the relationship between the other parent and the child...The Medea syndrome has its beginnings in the failing marriage and separation, when parents sometimes lose sight of the fact that their children have separate needs [and] begin to think of the child as being an extension of themselves...A child may be used as an agent of revenge against the other parent...or the anger can lead to child stealing' (5)."

Divorced Related Malicious Mother Syndrome

"Turkat would have done better to call this disorder 'Malicious Parent Syndrome' but be that as it may, this disorder describes a special class of alienating parents who engage in a relentless and multifaceted campaign of aggression and deception against the ex-spouse who is being punished for the divorce (6, 30). Contrary to Turkat, the author [Deirdre Conway Rand] has encountered several cases in which the father was the malicious parent...Discussing PAS by name, Turkat classified PAS as a moderate form of visitation interference as compared with Divorce

Related Malicious Mother Syndrome. The parent with the latter disorder uses an array of tactics including excessive litigation, alienating the child from the target parent, and involving the child and third parties in malicious actions against the ex-spouse. Lying and deception are routinely used. A malicious parent might arrange to have the ex-spouse investigated for use of illegal drugs at work or file a complaint with authorities against the ex-spouse's new partner. Malicious parents are often successful in using the law to punish and harass the ex-spouse, sometimes violating the law themselves but often getting away with it. Their efforts to interfere with the target parent's visitation are persistent and pervasive, including attempts to block the target parent from having regular, uninterrupted visitation with the child and from having telephone contact, as well as trying to block the target parent from participating in the child's school life and activities.

SAID Syndrome

(Personality characteristics of parents making false accusations of Sexual Abuse in Disputes)

"…the falsely accusing parents were much more likely to have been diagnosed by a professional as exhibiting a personality disorder including mixed, unspecified, histrionic, borderline, passive-aggressive or paranoid…Some of the false accusers were so obsessed with anger towards their estranged spouses that this became a major focus of their lives. They continued to be obsessed with abuse despite negative findings by mental health professionals and the courts, similar to what is found in cases of delusional disorder and Munchausen Syndrome by Proxy. The relationship of falsely accusing parents with their children was often characterised in the record as extremely controlling and symbiotic. Two were given a formal diagnosis of folie à deux between parent and child. Several exhibited extremely serious dysfunction, such as unpredictable bizarre behaviour, belief that they possessed supernatural powers and delusions of grandeur…"

Blush and Ross have come up with three psychological profiles for mother false accusers and a typical profile of father accusers (3, 26, 27). Mothers tend to present as 'fearful victim', 'justified vindicator' or to some degree psychotic. The 'fearful victim' presentation involves manipulation of social image around a specific theme to which others respond with sympathy and support, such as child abuse or spousal abuse. The 'justified vindicators' initially present as intellectually organised with a knowledgeable, even pseudo-scientific sounding agenda. Women in the third group present with a combination of borderline and histrionic features which interact with the stress of divorce to impair the mother's reality testing. Mothers in all three categories tend to be histrionic in presentation, so emotionally convinced of the "facts" that no amount of input, including from neutral professionals, can dissuade them from their perceptions. According to Blush and Ross, the typical profile for father accusers is one of intellectual rigidity and a high need to be "correct". By history, these men were hypercritical of their wives while the marriage was still intact, quick to suspect them of negligence and to accuse their wives of being unfit mothers."

THE DELUSIONAL PARENT

"Rogers refers to PAS in her report on five divorce/custody cases in which the falsely accusing parent, all mothers in this sample, suffered from delusional disorder (32). The children were subjected to undue influence to get them to accept the accusing parent's psychotic belief and concomitant rejection of the other parent in a severe PAS scenario. Where the child succumbed, a diagnosis of shared paranoid disorder, otherwise known as folie à deux, might also be made. According to Rogers, the first stages of the mother's delusional disorder were present to some degree during the marriage and exacerbated parental conflicts prior to the separation.

However, these subtle signs were not immediately discernible as a psychiatric illness and were only recognised in retrospect as the mother's symptoms became worse in the course of the divorce and its attendant disputes. One of the severe PAS cases reported by Dunne and Hedrick appears to be an example of the mother developing delusional disorder. The 'subtle' signs were expressed as suspicions during her pregnancy that the father would molest the child, similar to a case encountered by the present author in which suspicions harboured by the mother even before the child was born prompted her to abduct the child a few months later.

According to Rogers, the mothers who became delusional were usually the main caretakers for the children. In two cases, they were awarded custody during the first round of custody litigation, before more noticeable deterioration in their parenting capabilities had occurred. With continued custody litigation, the intractable nature of their mental illness became apparent and the court gave custody to the father in four of the five cases."

MUNCHAUSEN SYNDROME BY PROXY (MSP)

"...parents fulfil their needs vicariously by presenting their child as ill. In cases of "classical" MSP, parents repeatedly take their children to doctors for unnecessary, often painful tests and treatments which the physician is induced to provide based on the parent's misrepresentations. 'Contemporary-type' MSP occurs when a parent fabricates an abuse scenario for the child and welcomes or actively seeks out repeated abuse interviews of the child by police, social workers and therapists...MSP parents may change or come up with new 'symptoms' of the child so as to better elicit the desired response from a particular care provider or an institution offering specialised services. Thus the same child may be receiving attention simultaneously for fabricated sex abuse from therapists and public agencies who specialise in abuse.

...As with PAS, MSP is most often practised by mothers, although fathers and other caretakers are sometimes found to engage in the behaviour. MSP parents maintain their psychic equilibrium through control and manipulation of external sources of social gratification, including the child and care providers who serve children...

There are at least four different presentations where MSP and PAS overlap:
1. *an MSP mother may, during the marriage, add false allegations of abuse to the child's fabricated physical symptoms, thus precipitating the divorce.*
2. *where the MSP parent feels angry or rejected in divorce, manipulating the child's medical care and involving the child in false allegations of abuse may serve multiple functions including revenge, maintaining the symbiotic bond with the child and preserving the freedom to continue the MSP behaviour.*

3. a parent dealing with the losses and stress of divorce may respond with MSP type behaviour to obtain social support from the child and care providers.

4. an alienating parent may exhibit MSP type behaviour by manipulating the child's medical care for the primary purpose of furthering the alienation agenda..."

As in all of the above syndromes and however they manifest themselves under a syndromic name, it is grievances, revenge and avenging partners which place an immense burden and hardship on children. Their day-to-day lives are crippled under tremendous strains for which they are emotionally ill-equipped to either understand or come to terms with. They become virtual 'tools of revenge' used with great dexterity and forcefulness by one or both facilitating parents in an ever-increasing scenario of high conflict.

Deirdre Conway Rand puts this type of child into two categories:

the "overburdened child" and the "psychologically battered child".

The Overburdened Child

"Divorce almost inevitably burdens children with greater responsibilities and makes them feel less cared for. Children of chronically troubled parents bear a greater burden. They are more likely to find themselves alone and isolated in caring for a disorganised, alcoholic, intensely dependent, physically ill, or chronically enraged parent. The needs of the troubled parent override the developmental needs of the child, with the result that the child becomes psychologically depleted and their own emotional and social progress is crippled."

The Psychologically Battered Child

"...psychological maltreatment of children is more likely to occur in families where the atmosphere is one of stress, tension and aggression...psychological maltreatment can be viewed as a pattern of adult behaviour which is psychologically destructive to the child, sabotaging the child's normal development of self and social competence.

...Five types of psychological maltreatment are identified:

1. Rejecting: the child's legitimate need for a relationship with both parents is rejected. The child has reason to fear rejection and abandonment by the alienating parent. His positive feelings are expressed about the other parent and the people and activities associated with that parent.
2. Terrorising: the child is bullied or verbally assaulted into being terrified of the target parent. The child is psychologically brutalised into fearing contact with the target parent and retribution by the alienating parent for any positive feelings the child might have for the other parent. Psychological abuse of this type may be accompanied by physical abuse.
3. Ignoring: the parent is emotionally unavailable to the child, leading to feelings of neglect and abandonment. Divorced parents may selectively withhold love and attention from the child, a subtler form of rejecting which shapes the child's behaviour.
4. Isolating: the parent isolates the child from normal opportunities for social relations. In PAS, the child is prevented from participating in normal social interactions with the target parent and relatives and friends on that side of the family. In severe PAS, social isolation of the child sometimes extends beyond the target parent to any social contacts with might foster autonomy and independence.
5. Corrupting: the child is missocialised and reinforced by the alienating parent for lying, manipulation, aggression toward others or behaviour which is self-destructive. In PAS with false allegations of abuse, the child is also corrupted by repeated involvement in discussions of deviant sexuality regarding the target parent or other family and friends associated with that parent. In some cases of severe PAS, the alienating parent trains the child to be an agent of aggression against the target parent, with the child actively participating in deceits and manipulations for the purpose of harassing and persecuting the target parent. This is particularly likely to occur in what Turkat called Divorce Related Malicious Parent Syndrome."

Nearly all parents who have experienced part or full alienation from their children following splitting-up or high-conflict separation or divorce may be able to recognise one or even several types of syndrome from their own experience. Revenge is the key. Revenge is the name of the game by which the aggrieved partner will crusade for it selfishly and viciously through the children, forgetting that they are just that. Children.

Although I did not have the opportunity to 'use' my children as a facilitating or avenging 'tool' – as they were alienated from me right at the beginning of my separation – I did experience extreme and frighteningly malicious feelings of revenge against my former husband when he turned the children against me whilst pretending to have played no part in their alienation.

These thoughts surfaced on two occasions: when I gave up fighting for my children through the courts and when I was denied the opportunity to attend my son's funeral. My imagination took off into flights I never dreamed were possible. A burning need for retribution had probably been buried deep inside my subconscious mind for the previous two years, prior to my son's death, when the children had been manipulated into a frenzy of despising me.

After seven months of bereavement having had fires of rage inside me all that time, I experienced a vivid nightmare in which my son "survived" his accident. On waking, a violent and emotional storm of weeping shook me to the core with the brutal realisation that he was actually dead and that not only would I never see him again, I would never have the chance of becoming reconciled with him.

The releasing effect of this climax cleansed my mind and my spirit of revenge. This was followed by a feeling of complete acceptance of my situation. I felt relieved of an anger which had burdened me for far too long. It disappeared and has not returned since.

However tragic your own situation, acceptance of things you cannot change or influence may be crucial to making your life better. Acceptance of that simple fact may release you from many burdens.

A LETTER TO LEGAL, MEDICAL AND PSYCHIATRIC BODIES IN THE USA, UK AND EUROPE ON PAS

In July 1998 I wrote a letter, enclosing a paper on PAS to the representative organisations of the legal, medical and psychiatric professions in the United States, United Kingdom and Europe to see how widespread was their knowledge of it:

United States
American Law Institute
Philadelphia
USA

American Medical Association   [no reply]
515 North State Street
Chicago
Illinois 60610-4377
USA

American Psychiatric Association
1400 K Street, NW
Washington
DC-20005
USA

Europe
Institute for European Law   [no reply]
59 Dufourstrasse
CH-9000 St. Gallen
Switzerland

European Medical Association
12 Place de Jamblinne de Meux
B-1040
Bruxelles
Belgium

Association of European Psychiatrists
c/o Centre Hospitalier de Luxembourg
4 Rue Barble
L-1210
Luxembourg

United Kingdom
The Law Society
113 Chancery Lane
London
WC2A 1PL

The British Medical Association
BMA House
Tavistock Square
London
WC1H 9JP

Royal College of Psychiatrists   [no reply]
17 Belgrave Square
London
SW1X 8PG

On the recommendation of the British Medical Association I also wrote to:

Family Welfare Association
501-505 Kingsland Road
London
E8 4AU

I also wrote to the Divorce Court Welfare Officer who had prepared the report on my family.
July 1998

Dear Sirs

Parental Alienation Syndrome (PAS)

Dr. Richard Gardner in his book states that PAS is the systematic denigration by one parent of the other with the intent of alienating the child against the other parent. He defined this syndrome as a disturbance occurring in children who are preoccupied with deprecation and criticism of a parent and denigration that is unjustified and/or exaggerated. He describes these children as

"obsessed with hatred of a parent..."
"Many of these children proudly state that their decision to reject their father/mother is their own."

The criteria by which PAS is defined is outlined on pp24-25 of the enclosed extract.

· Do you know of any Case Law in this country on PAS?
· Can you advise on any research into it and how I may access it?
· Does your organisation have any policy on PAS?

The following organisations replied:

The American Law Institute
4025 Chestnut Street
Philadelphia
Pennsylvania 19104-3099

16 July 1998

In response to your letter I am enclosing the latest tentative draft of a chapter in the American Law Institute's Family Law Project.

This chapter deals with the law on child custody. It was tentatively approved by the ALI in May but will be somewhat revised before it is published in final form. It does not specifically deal with the syndrome you describe but it does advocate standards for allocating custodial responsibility which give high preference to the parents' parental roles prior to their separation.

The primary author of this chapter is Law Professor Katharine T. Bartlett at Duke University.

Elena A. Cappella
Deputy Director

American Psychiatric Association
400 K Street, N.W.
Washington DC 20005

25 August 1998

I am responding to your recent letter to the American Psychiatric Association regarding parent [sic] alienation syndrome.

The Diagnostic and Statistical Manual of Mental Disorders, Fourth Edition, does not include parent [sic] alienation syndrome.

I am not aware of any empirical, peer-reviewed literature on parent [sic] alienation syndrome. I would encourage you to contact your local library or medical school library for assistance in locating this type of information. Specifically, you may find it helpful to do a literature search using the databases Medline or Psychlit. Both of these medical databases may be accessed via the World Wide Web.

Laurie E. McQueen, MSSW
DSM Project Manager

The Law Society
113 Chancery Lane
London WC2A 1PL

13 July 1998

I regret that we are a private library for members of the Law Society and are not able to deal with your enquiry in detail. I enclose a leaflet (How to find information for a student project) and hope this will be of some help to you.

Practice Advice.

British Medical Association
BMA House
Tavistock Square
London WC1H 9JP

13 July 1998

I am afraid I have to advise you that the BMA is a professional association and trade union for doctors. We are not a clinical body and are unable to give advice on clinical matters of this kind. A potential source of advice in this regard is the Family Welfare Association.

Julian Sheather
Public Affairs

European Medical Association
12 Place de Jamblinne de Keux
1040 Bruxelles.

22 July 1998

Thank you for your letter which we have forwarded to the Global Alliance of
Marital Illness Advocacy Networks. I am sure that they are the most competent
organisation to advise you upon this matter. [No reply to date]

Dr. V. Costigliola

Association of European Psychiatrists
Centre Hospitalier de Luxembourg
4 rue Barble
l-1210 Luxembourg

13 July 1998

Herewith a brief response:

1. The AEP does not acknowledge or disavow any syndromes.
2. The AEP does not advise any research into syndromes.
3. The AEP does not have any policy on PAS.

Professor Charles Pull

Family Court Welfare
(my local Divorce Court Welfare Office)

25 July 1998

The Family Court Welfare Service are aware of parental alienation syndrome although we have no specific policy on it nor would there be a reason for us to do so. Knowledge of case law or research may best be accessed via a solicitor who specialises in family law.

Senior Family Court Welfare Officer

Family Welfare Association
501-505 Kingsland Road
London E8 4AU

21 July 1998

The FWA works with separating and separated parents in many of our children and families projects yet I would hesitate to suggest that any of our workers have encountered Parental Alienation Syndrome although, as part of much of our work, we work with families where parental hostility affects children's emotional and behavioural responses to their parents and the outside world.

As always American psychiatry runs ahead of our own in identifying syndromic conditions. I'm not sure that the situation described in the paper is different to anything that British psychiatrists encountered. It is, perhaps, more a question of terminology.

As to case law you are undoubtedly disadvantaged in seeking established precedent if you confine yourself solely to this condition. There is a wealth of case law on parents' implacable opposition to the other parent's wish to have contact with their children and, indeed, some case law on children's refusal to co-operate with contact arrangements in these cases.

Honor Rhodes
Director, Family and Community Care.

It would appear, from these responses that we have a long way to go on the road to getting PAS established in the minds of professional legal, medical and psychiatric people as well as ordinary people before it becomes established in our laws on child protection in the United Kingdom.

Those who have suffered its effects will feel it needs greater exposure and debate and that this is long overdue. Its classic symptoms, whether with a legally or medically recognised syndromic label or otherwise, are already being suffered by countless vulnerable children and parents who are powerless to do anything about it. If it is not recognised by the legal, medical or psychiatric professions in the United Kingdom and Europe, who will recognise it?

In the aftermath of post-divorce and splitting-up situations, revenge in all its diversity could reach epidemic proportions in the New Millennium without anyone fully understanding the reasons nor how to treat it nor how to counteract its adverse effects on our children's lives and their responses to it. This must change. The desire and the will to change should be paramount, for the sake of our children and their future well being.

Legal Recognition of Parental Alienation Syndrome by Solicitors and Court Welfare Officers

When my solicitor was preparing me for my last "appearance" in court, this time before a circuit judge, he spent some time instructing me on the various customs of court as well as the duties expected of all who were to appear in court. I was to be accompanied by him and represented by a very expensive barrister.

Although the questioning would come from my barrister – and the questions would be for me, court welfare officer and other witnesses to answer – the answers were to be given to the judge. So I should therefore turn slightly towards the judge, after looking at the barrister who was questioning me. My answers and those of my father, stepfather and brother – if called for questioning – were also to be directed to the judge and not the barrister.

My father and stepfather, unused to the ways of court, became nervous and stiff in their answers in the actual event, because they were trying to remember this complicated rigmarole, and they did not give an entirely natural performance as loving grandfathers denied access to grandchildren.

Deference, reverence, honour, veneration of the judge seemed to be uppermost in my solicitor's mind as he continued my education of courtroom culture. I half-expected that I should have to lay prostrate before the judge or lay palms at his feet. My feelings were that the whole court procedure was ultimately in place for people to pay homage to a judge who was there, in turn, representing Her Majesty The Queen and the State. The fact that I was there to fight for the rights of my children not to be emotionally abused, the fact that I had prepared a lengthy presentation of my case, became rather of secondary importance.

My solicitor suddenly paused in mid-sentence in the middle of my courtroom education, hesitating before speaking again.

"Now about your appearance, Mrs…"

"Yes?"

"I wonder if you could possibly wear… a skirt or a dress. The judge is a very old-fashioned type of man and doesn't really approve of women in trousers."

I immediately felt a rage boiling up inside me that the judge expected mothers to dress 'appropriately', that I was required to behave as an actor in a certain "character" part to influence the outcome to my advantage. Is this what the legal profession is all about? The judge would have passed judgement on me, on my fitness as a mother based simply on his opinion of what I was wearing. What about the 60-page report I had compiled on why my children had rejected me?

In the end it mattered little. I was convinced he had not even read the report but merely glanced at a few pages in the minutes before coming into court. A few weeks later, by a strange quirk of fate which life sometimes throws up, I met that same judge at a large party given by friends of my new partner and was even more convinced of his not being in the real world.

Many parents who recognise the symptoms of PAS, perhaps having experienced its effects within their own post-divorce circumstances but who have not necessarily heard of it until now, will wonder why it is that such a well-known concept, whether or not one gives it its syndromic name, is not universally known and acknowledged by everyone in the legal field but especially by Court Welfare Officers and social workers? Why are they not working to overcome its evil, pernicious effects on children?

There are many parents like me, who have eagerly seized on the huge body of evidence of PAS collated by professionals in the United States and Canadian legal domain and who have seen, at first hand, how many of its manifestations have been present in our own cases.

Possibly one of the answers as to why so few people outside of the United States know about it is that maybe we in the United Kingdom and Europe are suspicious of anything which we have not 'discovered' ourselves in our own country. How much exchange of information is there between legal, judicial and mental health professionals across the Western world which would be helpful to all parents fighting high-conflict divorce and custody cases to protect the interests of children?

One body of expertise in which most parents would like to find acknowledgement of PAS is that of judges and Court Welfare Officers on whom so much rests and with whom so much power is vested. When PAS is so glaringly apparent in an enormous number of cases where the alienated parent loses contact with children, it is difficult to find one CWO or solicitor let alone judge who knows that PAS exists or is prepared to acknowledge that it exists when CWO's are compiling reports for presentation in Court. Such reports are gravely important in deciding the future pattern of continuing relationships in a family. People's lives depend on the judicial system acknowledging the existence of PAS.

In my own case the judge granted me a temporary Contact Order and gave a set number of hours to the CWO for the whole case. Some of these hours in theory enabled her to interview my children with me without the presence of their father but the children refused categorically, for no clear reason other than not wanting to see me.

I told the CWO that I firmly believed their father had manipulated the situation to bring this about but my comments were misrepresented in her report as well as in court. As the CWO system is fraught with financial difficulties as well as being chronically under-staffed, she ran out of the hours she had been allocated by the first judge and was either unable or unwilling to pursue the matter with anything that could be described as 'vigour'.

A glance at the Family Court Welfare Service entries in the National Association of Probation Officers 1999 Directory (NAPO) reveals that many Divorce Court Welfare Officers have a large geographical area to cover. Many also work part-time.

It comes as an eye-opener to many divorcing parents that these officers are part of the National Association of Probation Officers. It may even come as a surprise to some parents splitting up that they - the parents - become part of a criminal institutional umbrella once divorce proceedings begin. Parents are now part of a judicial system covering criminal proceedings and illegalities of every kind. Members upholding the principles of law within this sacrosanct Establishment institution – judges, barristers, solicitors, court welfare officers - now figure in the lives of separating or divorcing parents. They are included in daily conversation and almost become a part of the family.

The appearance of such influential, venerated experts on, and members of, the criminal justice system in the lives of divorcing parents and their children must subconsciously send a message to children as well as to the world at large: someone, somewhere must be doing something very wrong if Family Courts, English or Scottish Law, solicitors, barristers, judges, divorce court welfare officers, and very large sums of money are involved.

The back page of NAPO's Probation Officers Directory proclaims its status as part of this criminal-fighting industry:

"The NAPO probation directory is the essential reference book for all those who work with offenders. It lists every penal establishment, specialist accommodation for offenders, services for drug misusers, problem drinkers and gamblers, sex offenders, victim/offender mediation services..."

The words 'Family Court' or 'Divorce Court Welfare Officer' however do not appear at all on the back page of the 1999 edition.

Why are Family Courts part of the criminal system? Why is the word 'Court' used at all? Why is divorce part of it? Is it because divorce still needs to be viewed as part of a medieval cross-examining adversarial system that needs presiding over by non-specialist judges? Is it commonsense for Family Court judges, solicitors, barristers and court welfare officers to be hostile?

Why are Family Court judges still mainly drawn from white middle-class male public-school-educated sections of the community? Many separating parents and legal professionals would like to see a broader cross-section of judicial people having specialist knowledge of the psychological warfare being employed by embittered or chronically enraged parents. Many admit to feelings of deep frustration that the Family Court and its current structure of incumbents do not seem much concerned that calculating and manipulative parents are emotionally abusing children. Lives are being wrecked amidst the cold-hearted apathy of the current system.

One or both parents may just want a simple divorce and a sensible allocation of children's time. Many may never have set foot in a court in their lives. They are suddenly thrust into a hostile environment of irrelevant rituals, rules and customs where both have to 'prove' which one is the better parent to claim 'ownership' of children through the Residence Order.

The battle then becomes primarily financial supported by Legal Aid and private savings. It doesn't take a genius to guess that it doesn't matter, financially, which parent gets the 'prize' of the children. Money-wise, there's only one winner of the twin purses of Legal Aid and private savings, and many children will become impoverished as a result of the high costs of divorce.

Dr. Richard Gardner confesses to being baffled, as are parents, as to why modern-day practices in divorce law and especially custody litigation

"are still using techniques that have their origins in the ritualistic practices of primitive tribes, ancient societies and the "Dark Ages"

and that these techniques are used in only a small fraction of present societies, namely England (and its former colonies) and the United States.

Dr. Gardner was even more surprised when interviewing some attorney friends and colleagues to learn that, when being taught at law school:

"Law students are presented with the adversary system as the system for resolving various kinds of disputes. Most are not even told about alternative methods of dispute resolution traditionally used in many other societies. Many, at the time of graduation, automatically assume that the adversary system is the best and the most efficient."

The Historical Development of the Adversary System
The Parental Alienation Syndrome

Financially, it seems to be in the best interests of the legal profession to leave the sleeping dogs of divorce lying where they are. The more acrimonious, the larger the purse.

Children and separating parents seem destined to continue to be heavy losers in divorce. Divorce should be a simple administrative procedure and as uncomplicated as possible.

Divorcing parents with children should have non-adversarial child-centred experts to guide them on children's best interests, to protect children from emotional abuse by manipulative parents. Procedures should be presided over by child health professionals in addition to a judicial expert, and rooted in sound commonsense to underpin children's best interests. Is this really happening in our current judicial system today?

LEGAL PROFESSIONALS WHO ACKNOWLEDGE PAS

Deirdre Conway Rand has collated some information about the increasing number of legal professionals who do acknowledge the existence of PAS and who wish to make it more widely known in their own field of expertise. However, these legal professionals are only in the United States. When will the legal profession in the United Kingdom and Europe follow suit? How many more years of suffering will our children have to endure as pawns in one aggrieved parent's need for revenge?

It is worth quoting at length from Deirdre Conway Rand's valuable research reported in The American Journal of Forensic Psychology, Volume 15, No. 4, 1997 to see that much is being done in the United States by the legal profession themselves.

"An increasing number of attorneys are publishing articles which recognise and seek to address the problem of parental alienation, variously using the term Parental Alienation Syndrome in the title, in the text or in the bibliography. California attorney Patrick Clancy posts his Points and Authorities for the Admissibility of PAS Testimony on his web site.

...Family law judges have been producing a growing body of opinions which discuss PAS by name or include findings of parental alienation without giving it a special label. ...A 1997 issue of The Judges' Journal included an article on managing visitation interference by Turkat who has been referencing Gardner's work on PAS for several years. Judge

Vernon Nakahara in Alameda County, California, spoke with author Deirdre Conway Rand about his opinion that judges need to be made aware of Gardner's work on PAS.

...A Florida attorney was the first to write about PAS after Gardner introduced the term in 1985. Palmer's article, published in 1988, described PAS as a strategy some parents were using to avoid their obligation to share parenting responsibility under Florida law. She discussed two legal cases...in which the judge opined: "The Court has no doubt that the cause of the blind, brainwashed, bigoted, belligerence of the children toward the father grew from the soil nurtured, watered and tilled by the mother. The Court is thoroughly convinced that the mother breached every duty she owed as the custodial parent to the non-custodial parent of instilling love, respect and feeling in the children for their father. Worse, she slowly dripped poison into the minds of these children, maybe even beyond the power of this Court to find the antidote."

...In 1991 A Canadian law journal published an article by Goldwater which strongly supports legal recognition of PAS. According to Goldwater, Gardner's 1989 book on family evaluation in child custody "is certainly required reading for the family practitioner and should be considered the source document on the phenomenon of parental alienation syndrome...Indeed, there is a moral failure in smugly asserting that children have 'rights' without taking into account their evident lack of autonomy and their material and psychological vulnerability to control and manipulation."

...In 1993, two articles were written by attorneys: one from New Hampshire and one from South Carolina. These articles took a practical approach to the special difficulties PAS cases pose to family lawyers, mental health professionals and to the courts.

...Since at least 1994, conferences of the Association of Family and Conciliation Courts have featured presentations on parental alienation. Gardner's concepts regarding PAS are often referred to and his books on PAS are listed in the bibliographies of handouts. Gardner himself presents at major conferences, for example, the Children's Rights Council

Conference in Washington, D.C. which is attended by mediators, psychologists and attorneys, who receive continuing education credits.

...Practising psychology and law in Wisconsin, Waldron and Joanis put forth the view that PAS was readily accepted not because it was a "discovery" but because Gardner succeeded in conceptualising and describing a familiar, complex, perplexing problem of divorce families which can have tragic consequences and is resistant to change.

...In Florida, Walsh and Bone practice law and psychotherapy, respectively. Their article on PAS, published in June 1997, appears to be the most recent paper [in 1997] on the subject by attorneys. According to these authors, courts in their state are not at all hesitant about making a decision regarding PAS...Four Florida case citations are provided in support of this assertion... "Make no mistake about it. Individuals with either PAS or a related malicious syndrome will and do lie! They are convincing witnesses and their manipulative skills may influence others to follow suit."

One of the above presentations and three of the articles mentioned above were co-authored by an attorney and a mental health professional. This may represent a trend of increasing collaboration between legal and mental health professionals who provide divorce-related services.

... extensive opinion by Judge Tolbert, published in the New York Law Journal in 1990, demonstrates the court's ability to match specific evidence with expert testimony on PAS by two experts, including Dr. Gardner who was originally involved as the court-appointed custody evaluator...Judge Tolbert opined that PAS is not so much an emerging area of expertise as a phrase pioneered by Dr. Gardner.

...Attorneys and parents also need to be held accountable. During his term on the family law bench, Judge Nakahara did not allow the common family law practice of the court relying on attorneys' representations as to what their client/parents and other witnesses would testify to if called. Similar to criminal cases, he insisted on live testimony so he could test the credibility of witnesses himself. At first, family lawyers in his courtroom were surprised that he expected them to show substantial proof in support of their claims and of the client's position. They were also surprised by his readiness to impose sanctions. Attorneys quickly learned that they needed to be more careful about their representations in Judge Nakahara's courtroom and that they would be required to back up their claims.

THE ROLE OF ATTORNEYS

...Waldron and Joanis observed,

The lawyer for the alienating parent has a difficult role. The alienating parent has collected evidence and invested time and energy in his or her role and has rectitude and certainty on his or her side, or so he or she believes. The alienating parent wants badly for the lawyer...to agree with him or her. The lawyer has been hired, however, for his or her knowledge and judgement." Waldron and Joanis recommend that attorneys who represent such parents should advise their clients to terminate the behaviour, in the best interest of their case.

...Similarly, Ward and Harvey assert, "It is incumbent on the attorney to sufficiently explore the client's motivation and the reality basis of the client's belief before litigation is undertaken.

PSYCHOLOGICAL EXPERTS IN DIVORCE

According to Sanders, attorneys representing target parents in PAS cases must retain a strong psychological expert. For judges unfamiliar with PAS, the expert's role in educating the court is essential. Otherwise, the judge will most likely make orders which are not strong enough to remedy the problem. This is especially true for judges who are unfamiliar with family law cases and do not have a particular interest in that area...Judges in some districts can be assigned to family law cases that they do not want and their motivation to read custody reports and be alert to alienation issues may be minimal.

...Sanders reported that when an alienated father is seeking custody, he should have a psychological expert who is prepared to give a strong opinion on the severity of the problem and the improbability that individual therapy for the mother or a restraining order against alienating behaviour will be enough to remedy the situation. It may be crucial to persuade the court that the child's relationship with the target parent cannot be repaired unless custody is removed from the alienating parent.

Waldron and Joanis identified the danger in PAS cases of the professionals who become involved becoming as split and contentious as the parents. Where possible, they recommend that mental health professionals who become involved work collaboratively with each other and with the attorneys. Depending on the circumstances, it may be possible for experts who enter the case on the side of one parent or the other to eventually become part of the case management team, especially if the court orders it...

...Ackerman and Kane included a section on PAS in the 1991 supplement to their reference work on psychological experts in divorce and other civil actions. In a subsequent edition, information about Gardner's work on PAS was included in the body of the text. Attorneys involved in difficult family law cases must be able to critically assess the qualifications and work of mental health professionals. Family lawyers may be expected to co-operate and participate in the selection of a custody evaluator, case manager or therapist for the child. Attorneys must also be prepared to probe the findings of mental health professionals and to cross-examine them."

The unfairness of inadequate, imbalanced or flawed representation by Court Welfare Officers of both parents in court, the unwillingness of the courts to legally acknowledge PAS, reflects forever on children and their future relationships with both parents. Judges should be actively informing themselves about PAS and its malevolent influence on the lives of children and all affected family member in order that parents like me should not rage at the injustice or the inadequacies of the Court Welfare Officer system of reporting their case.

This is what the legal and judicial professionals in the United Kingdom and Europe should be concerned with and not worrying too much about how parents dress for a court appearance.

Lorraine's Story

Your book made me realise I am not alone and we all share the same pain and heartache at the end of the day. I know how you must be feeling after your son died.

My middle son, Russell, who would have been 19 this year, drowned 9 years ago this July alongside his stepbrother, James and stepsister, Kathryn. Russell was found first then James. Kathryn was found three days later. I hope I never have to experience such a funeral again.

Hundreds turned out to say goodbye to the children. There's a plaque in memory of the children at the school they all attended. In the crematorium there's a bench with a plaque in memory of them too. Russell was a happy-go-lucky typical boy, always on the go. I still love and miss him dearly.

I also have a daughter who will be 20 in August and my youngest son was 16 on New Year's Eve.

I have not seen my children for years thanks to my ex-husband who has poisoned them against me. There's not a day goes by that I don't think about all my children. I love them all and miss them all dearly.

For years I have suffered with depression and still do. For all I have gone through I feel it has made me a stronger person. I still have a long way to go but it's nice to see the light at the end of the tunnel. Here's my story.

Fifteen years ago my first marriage ended in divorce after my husband left me for another woman. At the time my daughter, Kerry, was 5, my son, Russell, was nearly 4 and Lloyd was 20 months. When my husband left I had a lot of problems with Russell. He wouldn't eat or sleep and would sit on the stairs looking out the window, waiting for his father to come home.

A few months later I had a breakdown. My ex-husband agreed to look after our children until I was back on my feet. Once I was well enough to have the children back, he informed me he was going for custody as he did not think I was stable enough to care for them. I was gutted and couldn't believe what I was hearing. That was the start of years going back and forth from the Courts.

After a year my ex-husband won custody despite my hospital doctor, social worker, care worker, all speaking in Court and stating I was capable of being a full-time mother to my children. It made no difference. I was allowed access on a Saturday 10-6. I came away from Court heart-broken. In my eyes I had lost everything. My children were my life. I lived for them. My world revolved around them. Now here I was, all alone.

My ex-husband messed me around regarding access. I never had all my children together but was lucky if I had one of them. Two and a half years later my ex-husband moved house but didn't tell me he had just moved to the next street. I asked his neighbours if they knew where he had moved to but no one knew – that's what they were telling me. It took me two years to find him. In-between that time I had another breakdown. I went through hell and back during those two years of not knowing where my children were or if they were all right.

I took him back to Court and access was due to start on 21st July. On 14th July Russell drowned.

My world really did fall apart that day. What really hurt then, and still does to this day, is that I never had the chance to tell Russell I loved him. A year after Russell died I gave up fighting. I was physically and mentally drained. Every time I went to Court it was the same old story. Knock-back after knock-back. There was always some excuse why he didn't want me to see my children.

Two years ago in town, I came across Kerry and felt as if I had won the Lottery. Whenever I saw her after that, however, she ignored me until one day she did ask me why I had walked out on her and her brothers. She told me her father had told her. I tried to talk to her, to explain but she told me it was too late. Since then, Kerry has had a baby girl, Stephanie. She's just over a year old now.

Last year I was 40 and that was my turning point. It was time I thought about my self for a change. I'm now group organiser for Depression Alliance for sufferers and carers. I still live in hope that maybe, one day, I will be reunited with my children.

What "Ideal Age" Should a Child be When You Want to Leave?

Whatever the ages of your children when you leave seems to make little difference to their reaction. At a jazz concert I went to a few years ago George Melly told a joke about divorce – in very poor taste considering my own circumstances – but which has more than a hint of solid truth in the punch line.

A solicitor was making a great deal of money out of divorces. He had almost too many to deal with. One day a couple in their late-nineties came into his office.

"We want a divorce", said the wife.

The solicitor expressed surprise, after his initial shock, that at their very advanced ages they should want to bother at all. He tried to make them change their minds, despite wanting the business.

"Why not stay married?" he said. "It seems such a pity. After all, you have been together such a very, very long time".

"Oh, we've wanted a divorce for years," said the husband, "but we didn't want to upset the children. We thought we'd wait 'til they were dead."

If just some of the thoughts in this book are ever accepted as commonplace or commonsense, it might not matter whatever the ages of your children are. If the idea of a Family Union is ever adopted, any age could be "the right age".

Any age could be the "right age" for children to accept that both parents equally have their fair share of needs and faults.

Parents must learn to accept after their marriage comes to an end that both have a continuing and fundamental right to share in the lives of their children, whether those children live with them most of the time or part of the time.

Children should not be seen as trophies to be awarded to one parent through a Residence Order or as consolation prizes through a Contact Order or occasional access arrangements.

The parent granted the Residence Order should not view that award as a public prize or as recompense for a failed marriage for which he or she has no responsibility and has not initiated.

The 'consolation prize', the granting of a Contact Order or the lack of one, should not be viewed as public condemnation or a public flogging for the other parent who is then perceived as the inferior parent, having to bear the brunt of public denunciation for the failure for a collapsed marriage which then spills over, affecting the children's perception of that parent.

The right to share in our children's lives does not stem from any constitution but from a basic human instinct to want to continue to nurture our children and to promote their best interests throughout their lives.

Continuation of children's family life through contact with both parents after separation and divorce, should be of paramount importance to both parents and should be positively promoted and encouraged by both parents as well as by their extended family.

If you, yourself, have not initiated the separation or divorce, your bitterness, anger and resentment could spill over into a vast area encompassing your children, friends and family. The time span involved in clearing up messy issues could be lengthy, the costs in money alone might run into thousands and the consequences could drain the health of those involved for a very long time. It might damage you and your children forever. Is it worth it?

Don't let this happen. This is what divorce has done for years and years and years. It doesn't change anything: divorce will happen. Long-term relationships will disintegrate. Accept it as quickly as possible, maintain your relationship with your spouse or partner in the form of a friendship because, in the end, you will be richer in having played your part in keeping your children united with both parents as well as your extended family within your newly formed, uniquely special Family Union.

Don't let your anger or venom damage your children because you can't accept the ending of your marriage. Today, the only winner when we end a marriage is the legal profession which is enriched at the expense of our children.

In January 1998 [four months before my son died] I wrote to the Solicitors' Family Law Association in response to a letter they had written to The Times :

"I read your comments concerning recent editions of the BBC TV soap, "Eastenders".

You say the storyline implies "the law can do nothing to help people who fear they may lose their children if they walk out of an unhappy marriage" and you believe this focus is misleading. Your Association favours mediation or conciliatory action not only to prevent expensive legal battles but, more importantly, to protect unhappy, upset children and their parents.

Most people seeking divorce where children are involved would agree but, in reality, the law is not worth the paper it is written on. It did nothing to help me when I walked out of an unhappy marriage and lost my children: son and daughter twins aged 13 whom I have not seen for 17 months. Two adult sons now 21, 19, also refuse to see me.

Both my solicitor and barrister, with 50 years of matrimonial law practice between them, said it was one of the worst cases of revenge and manipulation they had known.

Court Welfare Officer's reports, Contact Orders, a legal order for a consultant child psychologist to assess the children's and my chances of re-establishing normal relations have failed: my children refused to co-operate, declined to see or to speak to me, returned presents, cards, and said they would like to "divorce" me as I was never a good mother anyway.

Having recently paid my solicitor's latest bill of £8,000, which included the divorce action and my barrister's bill of £1,100, I can tell you the "Eastenders" story line is probably correct: the law can do absolutely nothing to help a person who walks out on an unhappy marriage. The fear of losing children is very well-founded.

If I called on the combined experience of your Association, what advice could they sell me which would bring my children back? What suggestion does the Solicitors Family Law Association have on coping with daily feelings of bereavement arising from the separation from my children each day of the past 17 months?

My advice to your members is free: their clients should weigh up the emotional costs of enduring an unhappy marriage as long as possible if children are involved. The alternative is almost too painful to be bearable.

When my partner, who became my husband, settled my solicitor's <u>interim</u> invoice a few months ago, he sent his cheque enclosing the following note:

"On receiving your invoice I was reminded of a visit I paid with my parents to Ypres cemetery many, many years ago. One headstone in particular still stands out in my memory:

"In memory of Thomas Goodman
Born 1900
Died 1918
And for what?"

PRACTICAL ISSUES IF YOU HAVE ALREADY

LEFT HOME AND CHILDREN

If you have already seen a solicitor, a doctor or perhaps consulted advice bureaux, you will already have much to consider. You may have finally made up your mind to leave.

But if you have already left, having neither prepared yourself and your partner nor your children for any of the possible outcomes or issues discussed in this book, you may now find yourself stranded in the midst of a battlefield, a wilderness and perhaps have become estranged from your children.

Despite all your best efforts and those of third parties involved in mediation or conciliation, all initial attempts at a partial reconciliation between you and the children, all attempts at a rational solution between you and your estranged partner have failed.

Distressed as you undoubtedly are, try to understand the situation quickly, for the sake of your physical and mental health as well as your sanity. The children do not seem to want you in their life at this very moment nor in the foreseeable future. Although you will continue to fight this with all your will, all your resources and all your money, this unhappy situation must eventually be accepted by you, and the sooner the better.

Amidst the great unhappiness of separation from your children, you will be physically and emotionally over-stretched by the legal machinery moving, on behalf of you and your estranged partner, to organise separation or divorce litigation, Contact Orders, Residence Orders, in collecting personal property and perhaps being obstructed, or trying to reclaim precious mementoes, as well as all other related issues. All this will take up a huge amount of your emotional energies for a very long time, leaving you extremely tired, over-stressed, over-stretched and greatly disturbed.

But day-to-day life must go on and there are very real, practical issues to get sorted out and which you may possibly overlook in your intense misery. Some are vitally important, others less so but are necessary:

- Get a Change of Address form from the Post Office so your mail can be re-directed to your new or temporary address.
- Keep a diary or log book of happenings, of what your estranged partner and children have said to you or to other members of your family about you, if they have reported conversations. You may need to refer to these in a few months time. Some events and conversations unfortunately may even form part of future legal documents e.g. the early reaction of your estranged partner and children to your attempts at communication or reconciliation with them.
- If your children are of school age, contact their school, make an appointment to see the head, form teachers, or head of year so they are personally notified by you of the change in your circumstances and those of your children. Do not use it as a fault-throwing occasion. Be dignified, formal and calm. Confirm by letter any arrangements made between you and the school.
- Keep copies of all letters and correspondence to everyone.
- If the children do not want you to go in person to their school, and threaten not to take part in school activities if you do (as mine did), give the school a bundle of self-addressed envelopes so you can receive the school magazine or newsletter at least and keep yourself informed of what the school is doing. It represents some form of contact, however pitifully flimsy (it is all I retain of my children). The school are, in any case, obliged by law to send you written school reports of your children at appropriate points in the school year. Make sure the school has your correct address and telephone number at all times, particularly if you are in temporary accommodation.
- Contact the Inland Revenue so you can receive your Tax Self-Assessment Form. My ex-husband failed to return mine, I forgot about it because I was too involved with the legalities of ending my marriage and trying to get my children back. The Inland Revenue later fined me the statutory £100 with interest accruing two years later.
- Make a Will, properly formalised by a solicitor. You may be able to get Legal Aid for this or a friend or family member might help with financial assistance.
- Keep a diary, journal or scrapbook for your children of your positive, affectionate thoughts about them and your love for them. You will not feel

like writing something every day but write when you feel like it, even if it's just a word or two. They may not see it for many years but someday they will know you thought about them continually. Keep it up-beat and cheerful, let them know what you are doing, just ordinary, everyday things. They, or your grandchildren, may want to know more about you one day.

- Write letters to your children even if you don't post them, knowing they will be returned. Put them in a shoebox or filing cabinet in date order. Someone may read them one day but it will, in any case, do you good to write your thoughts, your hopes for their future. You need an outlet of this kind for your frustration and agony. Friends and family can only do so much or hear the same story so many times.

- Don't criticise your estranged partner to his/her friends or family. The advice of a prominent politician:, "never explain, never complain" is probably sound. People will make their own judgements in their own time and in their own way.

- Keep up Christmas cards to all friends, past and present, if you can afford to. The first Christmas you are apart is the worst: put a short but dignified note in with your card, explaining the factual change in circumstances, and expressing the hope all friends will continue the friendship with all of you, the children, your former partner and you. In my own case, all but three people continued their friendship and support with me. You will find out who your true friends are from now on.

- If you have school-age children, try to avoid being around school areas when it is going-to-school times and coming-home-from-school times, if you can. Separation is like an on-going bereavement. You will find yourself, as I did, searching the faces of children the same ages as your own, in whatever part of the country you find yourself in. It will not ease your heartache but increase it. You might stop doing this after a while and then feel guilty, feeling you have stopped caring. You do care, always, but you have to move on. Your children are always in your heart.

- Plan to do something constructive or practical on special days which have a significance for you and which you may not be included in now, Mother's Day, Father's Day the children's birthdays, Easter, Christmas. The first of these family-based occasions or anniversaries is always the most difficult one – a child's first birthday without you, your birthday without them, the first Christmas, and so on. Your heart will be heavy, you will feel desolate, the day will seem joyless but try to keep busy even if it's just walking or turning out drawers or visiting friends. Sitting around doing nothing is bleak. You will feel worse by the end of that day. If you can get out and walk until you're tired, you know you will at least sleep that night, more than you usually do.

- If you have a garden or just a window ledge, you might consider planting something which will mature year by year, even if you just transfer it annually to a larger pot. I am lucky enough now to have a good-sized garden. My four children have their birthdays within a 5-week period of each other. In early spring, just before their birthdays, two years after I left home and one week before my son died, I planted a four-leaf clover shape in box hedging, one leaf for each of them. This spring I await the pleasure of seeing different coloured tulips planted in autumn emerge from each leaf shape. On either side of my front door are two further box hedging panels, marking out the initials of my twins.

It gives me daily pleasure to see it all maturing, bringing me fractionally closer to children whom I know are also maturing, and nearer to my son who died on 20 May, tragically and ironically between the birthdays of his twin brother and sister on 17 May and the birthday of his elder brother on 29 May. I admit that plants in a garden are a frail link but they grow and mature like children. People whom I know well share the secret of my garden and understand how much I love and miss my children.

You may not believe it now but only time helps to ease the pain. "The sharp edges will become rounded in time" as someone said. It cannot be rushed. Time will help, in its own way, although you will be too unhappy to realise this at the time and will not accept it when people tell you, particularly those who cannot share your unique experience. Time will give you space to deal with pain in your own way.

There are professional and voluntary support groups (listed at the end of this book) who may offer genuinely sincere compassion or practical help of the kind you need. Some will have known similar agonies to yours and will offer you relief, borne out of their own experiences, as well as real optimism that you will, given time, find your way to a successful return to a full life without your children.

In my case, Compassionate Friends, a voluntary organisation formed 30 years ago by bereaved parents for bereaved parents, and MATCH, Mothers Apart from

Their Children, formed 20 years ago, gave me hope to go on when I was in dark despair (see addresses at the end of this book).

Families Need Fathers

I am reprinting in full a letter received from Stan Hayward, a Research Officer of Families Needs Fathers and someone who has done some (limited) research on Parental Alienation Syndrome. I contacted him in the hope that there may be some fathers apart from their children who might wish to consider contributing their stories to equalise or balance ideas expressed mainly by mothers in this book. You may want to consider his views alongside others and mine.

"I have now read your book, and am replying to it while it is still in my mind.

First of all, it is very difficult to get information about fathers. My survey on PAS with MATCH [Mothers Apart from Their Children] had more responses in a month than several years in FNF. I think this is due to the fact that men generally find it extremely difficult to talk about their feelings. I have on several occasions known men quite well yet only by chance have discovered that they had lost children through divorce or separation.

Again I am not sure if FNF cases would fit in with your book other than references to PAS, but even here it may well detract from your advice to parents who are considering leaving the family.

For fathers the situation is often different in that it is common for mothers to withhold contact as a means of getting money or property. I have yet to come across a case where a father withholds contact for this reason.

A mother may commonly accuse the father of sexually or physically abusing the children. Again, I have no cases of this for the fathers. From the cases I have the fathers will accuse the mother of incompetence, emotional instability and, in one case, of being a practising prostitute (sending me her call-girl card).

I have known cases of mothers who have killed their children because their new boyfriend didn't like the children. I have not heard of fathers doing the same. On the other hand about a dozen fathers a year in the UK kill their own children because the mother denies contact. I do not know of any mothers who kill their children because of blocked contact, though about 80 a year kill their own children due to depression.

It is obviously good advice to tell parents to plan their divorce/separation and make sure that they are not going to create insoluble problems in the wake of the split, but I do not think that is enough. In the cases you have quoted there seems to be two seemingly related elements, but which are not necessarily so.

In some of the cases the mother stays in the unhappy relationship until she meets someone she loves, and then moves. It means that she has the new love to look forward to but also has to take with her the burden of the separation. Both are so emotionally demanding that I cannot imagine how other aspects of normal life can be contended with. It would appear to me that the new love offers an escape route whereas the mother would be better off escaping into independence.

The aspect of "what others think" seems to affect mothers more than men. My experience is that other people generally do not want to be involved and, unless they are close friends or friends of the family, they prefer to ignore it altogether.

I will not detail it here as it obviously a huge subject, but basic advice I would offer is this:

1. *If you are contemplating leaving a relationship, make sure everything is in place to move. Make sure you have money to survive. Make sure you can live independently in the future. Make sure there are people you can turn to for advice on every aspect. Set up contacts with schools, doctors, and those involved with your children's welfare BEFORE you leave. Find someone you can confide in. This may often be someone not close but trusted.*
2. *Stay away from lawyers.*
3. *Don't assume that your new love will cope well. Experience with FNF shows that many mothers who leave with the children have unsuccessful new relationships and come back to the original father.*

4.   *If you have a new partner don't assume your children will like him.*

5.   *Try and stay on good relations with the father's friends and family if possible.*

6.   *Try to get your own friends and family to send your children cards, presents, etc.*

7.   *When sending gifts, include stamped cards and phone cards.*

8.   *Do not be upset particularly by hate mail. These are common. It is better to get these than nothing.*

9.   *Don't be pathetic.*

10. *Don't waste time writing letters and not sending them. When children come back (as they commonly do) they do not want to talk about the past. They act as though nothing has happened. I know many such cases.*

11. *Above all, plan your life. Have a diary that plans your week, your month, your year. Set yourself goals. Imagine your children turning up tomorrow. They would want to see you happy, fulfilled, and leading a life they would want to share. They would not want to find you drained, hostile, or begging for love.*

Also from your book and other sources, there is the common thread of mothers who devote their lives to their children who take it all for granted. Children do, and so they should. People have children for their own needs. My own mother devoted her life to me in every way. I left home as soon as I could at sixteen because I could not meet her emotional demands.

I know in every way what it is like to think of one's child day and night. Every conversation brings it in. Everything you look at somehow reminds you of the child. Everyone else's child seems to have something your child has. In my case my daughter lives a few minutes away so I often see people who know her. I even see the mother often though she walks past me. I work in the school my daughter went to and, mentally, see her in the class I teach. Her old teachers enquire about her, and I make suitable offhand remarks.

But I survive. I help other people's children. I work with Special Needs children who are deaf, blind, physically handicapped, brain damaged and, lately, Kosovo refugee children. I'm thankful my daughter is none of these. I don't see her now but one day I might, and am convinced that one day I will. In the meantime I lead a full life in every way. I send my daughter cards regularly. I send birthday and Christmas cards to the mother. I get friends to do the same. The mother knows that her hostility has not destroyed me. My daughter is reminded of me constantly.

In so many cases the custodial parent has problems of their own. They might become ill, they might need help in ways that the mother can offer. It is important that bridges are not burnt. Writing to the other parent offering help will sometimes get a response.

Though considering the loss of a child can be considered as a form of bereavement, it is closer to having an accident that prevents you doing the things you could do before. Adapting yourself to the new situation is better than putting it behind you, or hoping it will change."

Stan Hayward

TOM'S STORY

I left my former wife, Jackie, early in 1997 when our girls (Marilyn, Liz, Rosemary and Julia) were aged 8, 9, 15 and 17. It was a 19-year marriage and I played a full and active role as a father while Jackie had serious emotional problems that were a big strain on our relationship.

Since I left her, I have been denied any meaningful access to my children and Jackie continues to use the legal system mercilessly to stop me from being a parent.

In May 1999 I got re-married to the most wonderful woman, Sarah. We run a small business. She is enormously supportive and hardworking, enabling me to send £2,000 each month in maintenance to my former wife and children yet we are not allowed to have a relationship with my children.

Leaving – The Worst Day of My Life

I never imagined that if I left Jackie I would be prevented from remaining a parent to my children. I loved living with my children and leaving them at home was the most painful decision I have ever made.

I assured the children that I would make sure that, even though I no longer lived with mummy, I would spend more time with them than ever before. I told them I would speak to them everyday and they could speak to me whenever they wanted to. In the first few months I had some access to the children.

Jackie Denies Access

When I started seeing Sarah, however, Jackie became difficult about access arrangements and I was unable to speak with the girls on the phone. She blocked off all communication and my two older girls severed contact with me. Sadly, I now have no relationship with them.

I was deeply shocked. It was already a big adjustment getting used to not being able to see them everyday and I was aware that it was causing them emotional pain too. I wanted to sort out all arrangements amicably with Jackie but she just wasn't interested.

Court Welfare Officer (CWO)

My solicitor told me the CWO would give Jackie "*a stern talking to*". He was wrong! The CWO took no notice of anything I said to him and sided with Jackie.

The CWO arranged for me to meet with my two younger girls, Liz and Marilyn, at his office. He observed how comfortable the children were with me but nevertheless his report recommended that I should see the children just every Sunday on a visiting basis.

I had them for a few Sundays after that meeting. I was not allowed to bring them to my home or let Sarah accompany me. One day they stopped coming without any explanation from anybody.

Resolving the Finances

I decided to concentrate my energies on resolving the finances. I was told that if I gave Jackie everything she wanted I'd see my children again.

I gave her the family home (value £350,000), a lump sum of £39,000 and agreed to pay monthly maintenance of £2,000. I have never missed one payment.

18 months later I still have no contact and, despite writing to the children regularly, received absolutely nothing in return and no news from my children from anybody.

The Current Position

I continue to fight to have a proper relationship with my children through the courts. It is now nearly three years since I left Jackie.

Whether I will ever re-establish myself as a parent is extremely doubtful. Even if I succeed in getting a Court Order, the courts will do nothing to uphold it if access is denied. Jackie has made it very clear that a Court Order will not mean I will see my children.

The system is unbelievably unfair and rotten. It has helped my ex-wife use the children as a weapon. We will all bear the scars for the rest of our lives.

THE EQUAL PARENTING PARTY

This chapter has been written by Tony Coe, Leader of the Equal Parenting Party, a divorced father and Non-Resident Parent. Tony has occasional and limited contact with some of his children but is alienated from two.

He sets out some of the reasons why he and other parents formed a single-issue reforming political party (with a current membership of over 1,000) and discusses the way society in general and Family Courts in the United Kingdom in particular currently treat Non-Resident Parents after divorce and why there is an urgent need for reform, for the sake of keeping children in contact with both parents after divorce. The Resident Parent is the one with the winning hand. He/she is also known as the Primary Carer and is often supported by Legal Aid, the Family Court as well as society or "The Establishment". This unfair advantage and huge imbalance of power over the children usually ends with the children turning against the Non-Resident Parent. This person has no value in the eyes of society and, eventually, in the eyes of his/her children.

***

"Facts:

- Almost half of all Non-Resident Parents lose contact with their children within two years of divorce or separation.
- Fathers who lose their children outnumber estranged mothers overwhelmingly, but, as *Lost Children* demonstrates, it is happening increasingly to mothers.

RESIDENT PARENT (PRIMARY CARER, THE GATEKEEPER)+LEGAL AID+FAMILY COURT+ESTABLISHMENT

v.

NON-RESIDENT PARENT (PERSON WITHOUT VALUE)

Until they split up from their partner, parents remain blissfully ignorant that they can lose their children. Most people are probably unaware that the problem exists. Certainly I was blissfully ignorant. If anyone had told me three years ago that, as a result of my marriage breaking down, I would lose my children, I would not have believed them for one moment. When I say "*lose my children*" you may think I refer to custodial arrangements. I refer to losing access to them all together and ceasing to be their parent in every conceivable way except one: providing a monthly support cheque.

When my former wife and I separated I believed it would be best for our children to continue to live with her, their mother, in the family home. Spending long hours running my own business, I was the only breadwinner in a family of six and reasoned that, after my departure, we would share parenting time with our children on a fair basis. I sought to agree apportionment of time amicably with her.

Had I known I was going to be blocked without any good reason from seeing my children and barred from playing any active part in their lives, I would have acted quite differently. There was no clue at all then that, in effect, my children were going to be denied access to me for the rest of their upbringing.

In the last three years I have learnt about the manner in which our Family Court system deals with the children in divorce cases, circumstances that have made me determined to fight for reform. It has been astonishing to learn, too, that perfectly good, loving parents can lose their children even if they neither initiated nor wanted the break-up. Indeed, Family Courts appear to actively 'help' hostile Resident (custodial) Parents to alienate the Non-Resident Parent from children's lives without appearing even to be aware that they are doing so. It is one of most serious injustices of our time.

Be in no doubt whatsoever: if you become a Non-Resident Parent your relationship with your children, including whether you have a relationship with them at all, will be controlled totally by 'The Gatekeeper', the parent with custody. If The Gatekeeper is hostile, she/he can easily sustain a devastating campaign to denigrate you and can do so while saying all the time they are acting "*in the best interests of the children*". The Court will almost certainly back them and will treat you, the Non-Resident Parent, like a fly in the ointment.

- You will have to prove why you should be allowed to see your children.
- You will have to beg for crumbs of "contact" with your children.

Schools and doctors may be reluctant to provide you with information about your children.

In time your children will witness The Establishment and the Resident Parent ("primary carer") both treating you, the Non-Resident Parent, as a person without value and may find it easier not to see you at all. They may think that they, too, should treat you the same and may start to send hate mail, saying they never want to see you again.

Meanwhile, if you don't qualify for Legal Aid, you will be running up thousands of pounds in legal costs in order to achieve precisely nothing. The Resident Parent will very likely be supported by Legal Aid.

Faced with this situation many parents give up the fight and accept the loss of their children. The Resident Parent can then say to the children that you have abandoned them. You will be branded as feckless or selfish. If later, you recover sufficiently to reactivate your case for Access, the fact that you gave up first time will be used against you. It will be argued that you only want to see your children when it suits you.

You are damned if you do and damned if you don't.

If you are successful in getting a Court Order for Access it is not worth the paper it is written on. The Resident Parent may say the children were

'too ill', 'upset', 'didn't want to see you'.

If you manage to convince the Court that the Resident Parent is being bloody-minded, the chances are the Judge will do nothing about it. He may even respond by reducing your time with your children because *"contact arrangements are not working well"*.

These are the harsh realities of the current system.

"In the best interests of the children"

This severe learning process led me to get together with other estranged Non-

Resident Parents to form the Equal Parenting Party (EPP): a single-issue political party dedicated to fighting for reform so that children can keep both parents after divorce or separation. We believe both parents should be treated equally after divorce or separation, for the sake of the children.

Members and supporters include many parents who are also members of the excellent support groups referred to in this book: MATCH (Mothers Apart from Their Children), FNF (Families Need Fathers) and many others. Many heartbroken grandparents who have lost grandchildren as well as affected siblings, second wives and partners also support us.

Our intention is not to win seats in Parliament. We chose to form a political party similar to The Green Party's objective as a vehicle to raise public awareness of this growing problem of injustice. We fielded our candidate in November 1999 in the Kensington & Chelsea Constituency when Michael Portillo successfully fought his way back into Parliament. The campaign included distribution of nearly 70,000 leaflets to local residents.

EPP have come to realise that only reform of the legal system can provide an effective solution. The reforms we propose can be viewed on our website at www.EqualParenting.org or a copy can be sent to you (see address at end of book).

Having made excellent progress since our launch in July 1999, we acknowledge there is still a great deal to do. The task of convincing a judicial system that the present Family Court system is badly wrong, an institution populated by a legal profession perpetuating a billion pounds industry of petty disputes and technical cases that can drag on for decades, is an immense undertaking. But at stake is the future of our children who are being damaged needlessly by this lunacy.

The EPP will continue to fight to achieve reform with campaigners who have the courage and determination to do something positive for the sake of future generations of children. Many know that for their own children it's too late yet they are prepared to fight for future children and parents of divorce.

Many carry unspeakable pain, having lost their houses and businesses in fighting to see their children. The EPP consider that the legal system has let these parents down very badly but even worse it has betrayed their innocent children with the justification of "the best interests of the children". Is the needless banishment from children's lives of a good, loving parent really "in children's best interests"?

I don't think so.

THE AFTERMATH

After a traumatic life-changing event in our lives or having suffered a personal tragedy, there is an urgency in all of us to fiercely re-examine the event and the part we played in it. This strenuous self-examination of ourselves and our response to subsequent events with a what-might-have-been interrogation is, I believe, a necessary part of our progress towards healing deep wounds.

We need to lay the ghosts of the past to rest in order to go forward with our present lives. We wonder how we might have changed or affected that life-changing event. What might we, could we, have done differently to have avoided all the pain?

All parents who have lost contact with their children have reflected many, many times on their own life-changing circumstances, on what they did wrong, how it all might have been avoided. Could the pressures and the pains of the past have been re-arranged so the heartache of the present might never have happened? What might we have done to avoid it all?

The answer usually is very little. We took decisions rightly or wrongly with the life experience we had and the circumstances at that time. We might have been younger, less experienced, perhaps more imprudent or impulsive than now. We might simply have had no choice. But the soul-searching or re-living needed to reach that answer is for many of us part of our own healing process in learning to accept the loss of our children and, finally, in learning to live at ease with the consequences forever.

There are few happy stories, reunions or fairy-tale endings in this book but that is something most of us are managing to live without and, in doing so, have found that large-scale happiness is no longer necessary. What is essential now is peace.

Small amounts of joy can be discovered unexpectedly. Living quietly, having supportive friends, being at peace with ourselves and in harmony with others. The contrast with an earlier life of anguish or unhappiness eventually brings some contentment as well as occasional feelings of fleeting joy. In his book,

Couples Parting, Tony Gough talks about personal growth after separation or divorce:

"Without freedom it is impossible to grow. As human beings we have within us an almost limitless ability to grow and develop in all kinds of ways. What prevents us from seeing this is often found in the limiting factors in our past history: parents and parental figures, religious and educational teachers and our peer groupings. Stale and dead marriages are notorious breeding grounds for the restriction of our growth.

What we need to begin with, of course, is a dynamic – rather than a static – view of life itself. It is so easy to fall into the mistaken assumptions that life is planned out for us, it's all written in the stars, and whatever others dish out to us in our marriage is both inevitable and probably no more than what we deserve.

This is utterly self-defeating. There can be no personal growth while we suffer from such delusions."

Growth comes in many forms: personal growth, intellectual growth, the now limitless growth of one's previously restricted horizons. This brings huge satisfaction and excitement if we take it with both hands and use it but of course it almost goes without saying that we know, deep down, this is poor compensation if it is experienced at the grievously heavy cost of losing contact with beloved children.

EPITAPH – WELCOME HOME

As I was not allowed to attend my son's funeral, I arranged to have a Memorial Service for him at the church where he was baptised, in the town where he was born and where we lived for 16 years. He so longed to return to this place where he felt his deepest roots lay. I wrote this for the Service and would like to share it with you. Names and places have been omitted to protect my children's anonymity.

Having asked friends and family who are more capable than I to search books, poems, memories for words to describe who and why and how you were, I now place my jigsaw pieces face-up to try to complete an incomplete picture, to see what sense it makes, to make one whole picture, to give you life and form. Your helpless laughter, your irreverence, your quick-witted good humour, sometimes followed by ill-humour, the unselfish things you thought, said, did, the selfish things you did to safeguard and watch over your all-important family and your home.

Arriving first in 1976, you had 24 hand-knitted jackets and 36 pairs of booties to welcome you. Each stitch a stitch of love, said Nanna, great aunts and friends.

At 2, prophetically, you soon took responsibility for me, for your dad, for everyone – Daddy can't go to Scotland today, it's closed; I want to give the ducks brown bread, not white, to make them quack nice – and for your younger brother whose first words included "bossy" to describe you.

Busy, watchful, authoritative, "the gaffer" Granddad called you as you dug holes, fixed small cars, jumped on furniture, "helping" your Dad by chiselling out a channel of lathe and plaster wall in your bedroom, and showing your younger brother how to.

At 7, as first-born, you assumed the right to choose first: you wanted the right-way-up twin, so your younger brother had the upside-down one.

At 8, 9, you changed nappies, pegged out clothes, organised treasure hunts, invented games – "airmail" parcels delivered to friends three gardens away, made balloon water bombs, pass-the-parcels even at un-birthday times. You made indoor tents, outdoor hideouts, dugouts, and woodland camps when we visited Nanna and Poppa. Your brothers and sister needed no toys; they had your inventive, enthusiastic, generous time.

At 10, you were a home-loving, school-hating, project-making, fun-and-games boy, with a finely-tuned memory for blow-by-blow, frame-by-frame accounts of adventure films you'd enjoyed, and enjoyed relating ad nauseum, a mind for messy experiments – traffic light ice lollies which required you to open and close the freezer every two minutes so it resembled the North Pole – a hatred of libraries and reading but a love of Tin tin, comics, text books, visiting family.

At 12, you drove the car on Southport beach when we visited Granddad, kicked your way through new shoes every 6 weeks by playing football in your break-times, had a brief flirtation with the wearing of army jungle kit – "I bet you anything you won't let me have it" – and endured my irritation at your untidy, smelly bedroom. What wouldn't I give to smell it right now?

"I hate …[place we moved to], it's full of old people walking their dogs up and down. I want to go back home to …………."

At 14 – "am I old enough now to light the fireworks?" – a continuing and strong dislike of school, authority, homework, exams but a love of friends, friendship, cars, TV, computer games, the film "Back to the Future" and motorbikes.

"I hate … they share a brain cell when they're crossing the road. When I'm old enough, I'm going back home to …………."

At 16, cars and cooking matter but it's chiefly motorbikes, big motorbikes, powerful motorbikes plastered all over your bedroom wall.

"When I'm old enough, I'm going back home to …………."

At 17, ear-pierced, confidently reading out in front of 100 people the poem by Henry Scott Holland at my mother's funeral. Muscle-building equipment, the gym are new interests but you are ever helpful with diminishing family finances, being overly generous by paying household bills from your hotel waiter earnings. Our anxieties and burdens should not concern you but, with your caring nature, do.

At 18, 19, the motor vehicle engineering course at college engages you only if the tutor is more intelligent than you. It seems this happy occurrence seldom transpires. I nag you to complete assignments on time and with care. At Christmas and birthdays, you take infinite, painstaking care over buying just the perfect present for each of us. Your last present to me, Christmas 1995, "A Suitable Boy" by Vikram Seth, I treasure.

"I'm going to get a job and go back home to ...."

At 20, you are still watchful, as always, of your parents' failing marriage. Even you cannot mend this. It makes you angry that you can't. Fiercely, ferociously closing ranks around a newly formed family unit, you shut me out with a grim, steely determination as I leave, protecting, watching over them all.

At 22, you get that job in .... and at last acquire your big dream machine, my lovely dream boy. How magnificent you looked, how powerful, how supremely proud as you lay in your red leather gear, my home-loving, family-protecting, motorbike boy, and finally came home to ....

Welcome home.

Some organisations which may offer help or advice
(In alphabetical order)

Self-help groups and voluntary organisations proliferate and change addresses or telephone numbers so rapidly that it is best to go to your local library and check on which ones are currently operating. See also Helplines at the beginning of your Yellow Pages telephone directory.

ChildLine
2nd Floor Royal Mail Building
Studd Street
London N1 0QW. www.childline.org.uk

(Young people can ring ChildLine free, 24 hours a day on 0800 1111)

ChildLine, a registered charity, operates a confidential telephone help line for young people in distress. It listens without blaming or criticising and takes young people's problems seriously.

Dawn Project
95-99 Effingham Street
Rotherham
South Yorkshire
S65 1BL
Tel: 01709 512436

Their aims are to gather information on all examples of work with children throughout the UK, to publicise best practice, to determine best forms of work with the children of family breakdown. The Dawn Project deals with issues related to the painful experiences of children as well as adults. CareZone is one example of the work being done in this direction and on ShareZone web site children are invited to share their problems.

Divorce Recovery Workshop
National Phone No 07000 781889
email drw@drw.org.uk www.drw.org.uk

UK nationwide self-help group run by volunteers who have attended the workshop. There are no 'experts' but all those present will have personally experienced a relationship break-up. DRW is a course that helps an individual deal with the emotional trauma of a relationship that has irretrievably broken down.

Equal Parenting Party

38-40 Gloucester Road, London,
SW7 4QU.
Tel: 020 7589 9003
Fax: 020 7584 4230
e-mail: tonyC@EqualParenting.org

EPP was launched in July 1999 as a single-issue political party to spearhead public support for reforms to end the tragedy of children losing or becoming alienated from one parent after a separation or divorce. EPP always needs active campaigners and always needs money. Donations and new members are welcome.

Families Need Fathers

134 Curtain Road
London
EC2A 3AR

A registered charity formed in 1974, FNF provides advice, heavily father-oriented, on children's issues for separated and divorced parents and are principally concerned with the problems of maintaining a child's relationship with both parents during and after family breakdown.

Family Law Association

Tel: 0171 813 5300

Family Welfare Association

501-505 Kingsland Road
London E8 4AU
Tel: 0171 2546251

The FWA is a registered charity working with separating and separated parents in many children and families projects.

Gingerbread
16-17 Clerkenwell Close
London
EC1R 0AA
FREEPHONE: 0800 018 4318

An organisation for lone parents. They provide self-help groups for lone parents and offer an advice line.

The Grandparents Federation
Moot House
The Stow
Harlow
Essex
CM20 3AG
A support group for grandparents who have lost contact with grandchildren following family break-up.

Marriage Care
Clitherow House
1 Blythe Mews
Blythe Road
London
W1 0NW
Tel: 0171 371 1341
Help line: 0345 573921

Marriage Care's practice is informed by faith, its purpose is to help people prepare for, achieve and sustain successful marriages and to support them should their marriages break down. An overriding concern remains the health and well being of the individual. Central to this is their belief in marriage as the prime relationship through which people can mature and grow. Marriage Care reports to the Lord Chancellor's Department, its core funder.

MATCH (Mothers Apart from Their Children)
BM Problems
London
WC1N 3XX (send sae)

A nation-wide self-help group for women living apart from their children, offering unconditional and non-judgemental understanding, support and friendship.

NCH Action for Children
85 Highbury Park
London
N5 1UD
Tel: 0171 2262033

NCH Action for Children is one of Britain's foremost children's charities, caring for 30,000 children, young people and their families through over 520 projects nationwide including counselling and mediation services. Contact the head office to find out whether a local project operates near you.

National Council for the Divorced and Separated
168 Loxley Road
Malin Bridge
Sheffield
S6 4TE
Tel/Fax: 0114 231 3585 e-mail pat@ncds.org.uk

Formed in 1974, NCDS is a voluntary non-profit making organisation controlled by a national executive committee and is primarily interested in promoting an active social life for their members. Membership is available to all divorced, separated, widowed people.

National Family Mediation
9 Tavistock Place
London
WC1H 9SN
Tel: 0171 383 5993

A registered charity formed in 1981, NFM is a non-governmental association of 60 local family mediation or conciliation services, which offers help to couples, married or unmarried, who are in the process of separation or divorce.

The National Stepfamily Association

3rd Floor, Chapel House
18 Hatton Place
London
EC1N 8RU
Tel: 0171 209 2460
Help line (Parentline) on 01702 55 99 00
Web site: http://www.webcreations.co.uk

A registered charity, they offer advice and information to people in stepfamilies, operating a help line, staffed by volunteer parents trained in the issues callers may bring. It operates from 9am-9pm Mondays to Fridays and 1-6pm Saturdays. They also sell a range of books and leaflets on the pressure points that affect people in changing families.

National Association of Child Contact Centres (NACCC)

Minerva House
Spaniel Row
Nottingham
NG1 6EP
Tel: 0115 948 4557 Fax: 0115 941 5519

NACCC is a national charity supporting over 250 member centres throughout England, Northern Ireland and Wales. These are neutral meeting places where children of separated families can enjoy contact with one (or both) parents, and sometimes other family members, in a comfortable and safe environment when there is no viable alternative. They aim to provide short-term help and support towards establishing meaningful contact between child and visiting parent.

Parentline

Westbury House
57 Hart Road
Thundersly
Essex
SS7 3PD
Tel: 01268 757077

Rape Crisis Centre
Tel: 0171 837 1600

Relate
Herbert Gray College
Little Church Street
Rugby
CV21 3AP
Tel: 01788 573241 www.relate.org.uk

Relate is the UK's largest couple and relationship counselling service. In 1997 it saw 70,000 cases at its 121 centres in England, Wales and Northern Ireland. Look at the Contents page of your local Yellow Pages telephone directory for local help line or contact the head office on the above number.

Reunite
The National Council for Abducted Children
PO Box 4
London
WC1X 3DX
Tel: 0171 404 8356
Its main objective is to provide support and information on the issue of child abduction.

Shared Parenting Information Group
85 Dunscombe Street
Walkley
Sheffield
S6 3RH (send sae)

The SPIG was formed to encourage and promote the continuation of parenting after family breakdown. They believe "it is of vital importance that, wherever possible, both parents should continue to fulfil their responsibilities by retaining a strong positive parenting role in their children's lives, with the children actually spending substantial amounts of time living with each parent." [extract from their Submission to the Lord Chancellor's Department consultation exercise: Procedures for The Determination of Paternity and on The Law on Parental Responsibility for Unmarried Fathers, May 1998].

With Dignity

104 Earls Road
Nuneaton
CV11 5HP
Tel: 01203 350312/01203 397947 (Help line 9am-midnight 7 days a week)

A registered charity and the first organisation of its kind in the UK whose aims are to help, support and befriend people confronted with suspected or confirmed adultery of their partner or those still coming to terms with the loss of their partner through divorce.

Women's Aid National Help line

Tel: 0345 023468

Advice for women suffering domestic violence.

The Samaritans

Available 24 hours a day on 0345 909090 if you are in crisis. Look at the Contents page of your local Yellow Pages telephone directory for help lines of local counselling organisations.

The Compassionate Friends

53 North Street
Bristol
BS3 1EN
Tel: 0117 9 539 639

The Compassionate Friends was founded in 1969. It is now a nationwide organisation of bereaved parents who have experienced heartbreak, loneliness and isolation, following the death of their children. The Compassionate Friends offers no 'cure' but comfort, support and encouragement, and the realisation that, after the pain and turmoil, life will come to have meaning once more.

Others Addresses

Dr. R. A. Gardner, MD
Clinical Professor of Psychiatry
Division of Academic Child Psychiatry
Columbia University
Morningside Heights
New York NY 10027
USA

Peggie Ward, PhD
Foundation Medical Partners
280 Main Street, Suite 310
Nashua
New Hampshire 03060
USA

John E. Dunne, M.D.
Child and Adolescent Psychiatry
South Lake Professional Group
Renton Plaza Building
1400 Talbot Road South, Suite 203
Renton
Washington 98055
USA

Useful Books for Professionals

The Parental Alienation Syndrome, 2nd ed., Richard A. Gardner, M.D. (Creative Therapeutics Inc., New Jersey, USA, 1998) [available from Smallwood Publications, The Old Bakery, Charlton House, Dour Street, Dover, Kent CT16 1ED Dover, UK]

For Richer, For Poorer: Mothers Confront Divorce, Demi Kurtz (Routledge, USA, 1999)
"...divorced mothers of different classes and races ...describe leaving their marriages, managing their families on reduced incomes, negotiating with their

ex-husbands for resources and custody and visitation agreements, and rebuilding their own lives and those of their families. Many women experience serious conflicts with their ex-husbands over resources, custody and visitation during this process, and some are fearful. [extract from Routledge publicity]

The Handbook of Separation and Divorce (Routledge, London, 1999)
...principally concerned with the financial consequences of marriage breakdown in England and Wales, recognises that everyone who separates or divorces will be the poorer and recommends that those who can face mediation should undertake it while at the same time ensuring they can get independent legal advice. Essential reading for social workers and health professionals as well as the general reader and those going through, or considering, divorce or separation. [extract from Routledge publicity]

Family Transformation Through Divorce and Remarriage: A Systemic Approach, Margaret Robinson (Routledge, London, 1999)
One marriage in three is likely to end in divorce. One in seven families is likely to be a single-parent household. One in eight families is probably a stepfamily. ...Many of the children of these families will be referred to child and family guidance clinics with divorce-related problems, while others, whose parent(s) are often living near the poverty line, may be considered to be seriously at risk through neglect or abuse.

Useful Books from Relate for Parents trying to stay together

For those whose marriage or relationship is in crisis and who are seriously attempting to mend it, the following books are available from the Relate Bookshop, Herbert Gray College, Little Church Street, Rugby CV21 3AP (Tel: 01788 551424) or your local library may be able to get you a copy.

The Relate Guide to Better Relationships
The Good Marriage
Couples in Crisis
The Relate Guide to Staying Together
Crunch Points for Couples
Stop Arguing, Start Talking
Families and how to survive them

Saving the situation
How to love and be loved
Living together
You just don't understand
That's not what I meant
Out of work – a family affair
To love, honour and betray
Partnering

USEFUL BOOKS FOR SEPARATING PARENTS AS WELL AS THEIR CHILDREN

The Family through Divorce: How you can limit the damage. A Guide to the new Divorce Laws, Roger Bamber and Janet Reibstein (Thorsons, London, 1997)
Divorce: What About The Children? (Relate).
Me and My Family (Cambridge Family & Divorce Centre).
Teenagers & Divorce (Relate).
Teenagers & Sexuality, John Coleman (The Trust for the Study of Adolescence).
Teenagers & Divorce, John Coleman.(The Trust for the Study of Adolescence).
Teenagers & Step-parents, John Coleman (The Trust for the Study of Adolescence).
What About... ME?, Joan Collinson (Family Conciliation, Northumberland).
Helping Children Cope With Separation, Claudia Jewett (Batsford). £15.95.
Child Care Policy & Practice (Batsford).
Groups for Children. Maybel King (Family Mediation, Scotland).
Chasing Rainbows, Brynna Kroll (Russell House). £14.95.
Children in the Middle, Ann Mitchell (Tavistock Publications). £14.99.
Children & Divorce. Roger Smith (National Society, Church House).
Caught in the Middle, Alys Swan-Jackson (Piccadilly). £5.99.
Helping Children Cope With Divorce, Rosemary Wells (Sheldon). £6.99.
Straightforward Guide to Divorce and the Law, Alexander Lowton (Straightforward Press, 1996)
Separation and Divorce, Craig Connellan (ed), Olivia Coles (Independence Educational Publishers, 1999)
How to survive divorce, Roy van den Brink Budgen (How to Books, 1994)
Dinosaurs Divorce, Laurene Krasney Brown and Marc Brown (Collins, London, 1987)

Divorce Casualties: Protecting Your Children from Parental Alienation, Douglas Darnall, What to Tell the Kids About Your Divorce, (The American Bar Association)
My Parents are Getting Divorced, Darlene Weburne

can all be obtained from Divorce Source, Inc. P.O. Box 1580, Allentown, PA 18105-1580, USA. Mail Order/Fax Order: 610-770-9342)

USEFUL BOOKS FOR SINGLE PARENTS

Successful Single Parenting, Mike Lilley (How to Books at £8.99). How to combine bringing up children with your other life goals.
Lone Parent Survival Guide, Sue Slipman (Boatswain Press). £1.95. All you need to know to survive as a lone parent.
Journey Through Single Parenting, Jill Worth (Hodder & Stoughton). £6.99. A practical guide to finding fulfilment.

USEFUL BOOKS FOR STEPFAMILIES

Step-Parents and Their Children, Stephen Collins (Souvenir Press). £6.95.
Successful Step-Parenting, James D Eckler (Better Way Books). £6.95.
The Relate Guide to Second Families, Suzie Hayman (Vermillion). £9.99.

USEFUL BOOKS FOR TEENAGERS

Fiction
Breaking Point, Anne Bailey (Faber Teenage). £4.99.
It's Not The End Of The World, Judy Blume (Macmillan). £3.99.
The Divorce Express, Paula Danziger (Mammoth). £2.99.
Step By Wicked Step, Ann Fine (Longman). £4.95.
Flour Babies, Ann Fine (Puffin). £4.99.
Goggle-Eyes, Ann Fine (Puffin). £3.99.
Madame Doubtfire, Ann Fine (Penguin). £4.99.
Please Come Home, Michael Hardcastle (Faber & Faber). £4.99.
Stepping Out, Clare Harding (Pan). £3.50.

Worlds Apart, Jill Murphy (Walker). £3.50.
Henry's Leg, Ann Pilling (Puffin). £4.99.
The Suitcase Kid, Jacqueline Wilson (Yearling). £3.50.

Non-Fiction
Changes (Plymouth Family Conciliation).
It's Not Your Fault, Rosemary Stones (Piccadilly). £5.99.
This book talks about what to do if parents divorce.

BIBLIOGRAPHY

The American Journal of Forensic Psychology, Volume 15, Number 3, Deirdre Conway Rand, The Spectrum of Parental Alienation Syndrome (Part 1), 1997
Attachment Theory for Social Work Practice, David Howe, School of Health and Social Work, University of East Anglia, Norwich (Macmillan Press Ltd., 1995)
Breaking up without cracking up: Reducing the pain of separation and divorce, Christopher Compston (HarperCollins, London, 1998)
Caught in the middle: Protecting the children of high-conflict divorce
Carla B. Garrity, Mitchell A. Baris (Jossey-Bass Inc., California, 1997)
The Complete Guide to Living Together, Tobe Aleksander (Headline Publishing plc, London, 1992)
Couples Parting, Tony Gough (Darton, Longman and Todd, London, 1992)
Divorce Hangover, Anne N. Walther (Cedar, 1992)
Dinosaurs Divorce, Laurene Krasney Brown and Marc Brown (Collins, London, 1987) [a picture book for very young children]
Family Wars, Peggy Ward and J. Campbell Harvey
http://homepages.iol.oe/~pe/PAS_Report.htm
Post Divorce parenting-rethinking shared residence, Child and Family Law Quarterly, Vol.8, No. 3, 1996, Arthur Baker and Peter Townsend.
Stop Arguing, Start Talking, Susan Quilliam (Vermilion, London, 1998)
The Relate Guide to Better Relationships, Sarah Litvinoff (Vermilion, London, 1998)
The A-Z Reference Book of Syndromes and Inherited Disorders, Patricia Gilbert (Stanley Thornes Ltd., Cheltenham, UK, 1997)
The Family through Divorce: How you can limit the damage. A Guide to the new Divorce Laws, Roger Bamber and Janet Reibstein (Thorsons, London, 1997)
The Parental Alienation Syndrome, 2nd ed., Richard A. Gardner, M.D. (Creative Therapeutics Inc., New Jersey, USA, 1998)

Divorce Casualties: Protecting Your Children from Parental Alienation, Douglas Darnall, What to Tell the Kids About Your Divorce, (The American Bar Association)
My Parents are Getting Divorced, Darlene Weburne
How to Divorce as Friends (4 Audio Cassettes Running Time: 110 Minutes), Bill Ferguson

can all be obtained from Divorce Source, Inc. P.O. Box 1580, Allentown, PA 18105-1580, Mail Order/Fax Order: 610-770-9342)

If you have any comments on LOST CHILDREN or would like to contribute a personal story that might help another family whose parents are thinking of separating, please write to Velvet Glove Publishing. Your text should be not more than 500 words and may be considered for publication in one of two follow-up books planned for next year:

Parents, Professionals and PAS
Children's Voices: The right way to split up

NB If you are under 18, please state your age. You do not have to use your real name.

If this is a library book, please photocopy this page.
To order a copy of this book please enclose a cheque for £8.99 per book plus £1.00 per each copy for postage and packing, payable to Velvet Glove Publishing. Send to Velvet Glove Publishing, PO Box 30617, London E1W 1GP.

Name _____

Address _____

_____

_____

Postcode_____

No. of copies _____ Price_____